# The Pursuit

# The Pursuit

## Book I
## The In-Between

John Naylor

www.thepursuitbooks.com

To the woman I love;
my wife, Tracey

# 1

# The End

In most ways Trevor would be considered a good man, at least that's what he told himself. Hardworking and resourceful, he had positioned himself at the threshold of upper management for a well respected telecommunications firm. Not a bad accomplishment for someone still months away from his 45th birthday. He owned a nice house, in a nice neighborhood, in a very nice town in northwest New Jersey. It was one of those towns so well endowed their greatest concern seemed to be protecting athletic fields from too much activity during periods of bad weather. He drove a somewhat pricey SUV 27.3 miles to work each day and his wardrobe was only limited by his disdain for clothing stores. He hired a painting contractor from time to time, depending on which rooms needed primping, and a landscaping crew to cut the lawn, but he always raked his own leaves. Trevor had even managed to save enough money, aside from his retirement investments, to purchase a boat: a 33 foot Sea Ray that was barely a year old. He wanted desperately to get it back in the water now that Spring was warming. There was something about being on water that calmed Trevor's soul.

He thought himself a kind and charitable man, serving dinner to the homeless each Thanksgiving Eve, and refraining from the abuse of both bottle and his wife. Most would have expected such abuse, especially after the things he witnessed as a child. The cold and calculated silence, the torrent of negative comments and gestures, the aggressive and threatening behavior, and the moments of drunken rage, were all part of the world in which Trevor was nurtured. He couldn't fully understand it then, but he accepted it, never aware that things could be different, that things could be better. His mother had tried with all her might to shield he and his siblings from the abuse, but she was a victim too, and often ran out of strength long before her husband. It was during those days that Trevor stepped up to care for his younger brother and sister, regardless of whatever pain he might be feeling, and learned a great deal about being strong. Through the years he developed an intolerance for the behavior of his father, and he never laid a violent hand upon his wife.

But much like the rest of humanity, Trevor was not quite perfect. It was also true he had made a couple of bad mistakes along the way, the not so good side of Trevor.

There was an almost two year affair with an attractive lawyer from Codby and Barnes before he turned 30. It ripped Cindy apart and drove her back home with her parents for a couple of months, but Trevor was still young and selfish in those days, and the other woman had practically thrown herself at him. He had grown up a lot since then and there was no way he would ever repeat that behavior. These days he barely looked at other women, and he had learned long ago how to keep his flirtatious words to himself.

There was also an arrest back in '02 when his blood alcohol level provided ample reason why he very abruptly parked his car into

4

the trunk of a tree. Somehow he was able to redeem himself, vowing never to drink beyond excess again. Although six months without a driver's license was inconvenient, it did provide great motivation to stay sober, and for more than a decade since he held his ground by keeping dry.

But Trevor's life was not all about redeeming failures. He was remotely aware of a darker slice of his being, filled with the same kind of pain and despair that hits most men in their forties. The realization that they will not shake the world. The sad inventory of broken relationships and missed opportunities. The cold and sobering truth that each of us really wants so much more than this world will ever offer. The sting can be unbearable, driving most to the drug of their choice as they desperately attempt to numb away the pain. Materialism. Adultery. Bitterness. Drugs. Alcohol. Trevor, at this point in life, believed himself too strong to stumble. He also thought, unlike most, he did a pretty good job of hiding his shortcomings.

There was, however, more at work in Trevor's life than he was aware of, and a surprise came one day that caused him to question the mastery he held over his domain. As he looked into his wife's eyes, she spoke words he had never heard her say before, words he never imagined she would say.

"I want to go to church tomorrow."

A nagging sensation chewed at his stomach. Church, he thought, was for the weak and needy, a hiding place for those who struggle in life. He knew God was a lie, a convenient invention handed down from primitive man to explain away difficult circumstances, while simultaneously offering false hope to the hopeless. He also knew the Bible was a fairy tale concocted by men with dubious motives, attempting to subjugate the masses. He wondered how any educated person could buy into outlandish accounts of a sea being split in two or a carpenter rising from the dead. After the words left her mouth, he pondered for a moment in the area of his brain where no one was allowed to enter.

"Are you serious?" he asked, carefully studying her face, half expecting a grin to form and break into a giggle.

"Yes I am. Beth is going to meet me there at 9:15 in case you want to join us." There was no smile, not even a smirk. In fact, her face was childlike in its naiveté, almost waiting for him to concede and join them, like a chess master in forfeit. Trevor slowly, reluctantly, realized that his wife was serious.

His mind started churning. It was true they had been married in a church, but that was more about tradition and saving money than anything else. There was also the token visit every Christmas Eve when some random group of people would attempt to portray a new angle on a two thousand year old fable.

*No one really believed any of it, did they?*

Trevor considered church to be about trying to make people feel good or bad so they could make it through another week, the same way a recovering alcoholic tries to get through each day. It was a place filled with self-righteous fools, ceramic smiles, and a shameless thirst for more money. It was no place he wanted himself, or his wife, to be.

The phone rang and Trevor hurried to grab it. He was hoping

to buy some time to better analyze the present situation. He thought the incoming call might provide a good distraction.

"Hello," he said, listening to only a few words before reaching out his arm and handing the receiver to his wife. It was his mother-in-law. Once Cindy had the phone in hand, Trevor hustled out of the room and down the steps, ignoring her signal to wait.

Making his way outside he followed the front walkway across the house and toward the garage where he found the perfect alibi for his exit; garbage. Trevor took hold of the large plastic bin and started wheeling it down the driveway, contemplating why Cindy might have reached such a dramatic change of heart. He wondered if some bizarre cult had found inroads with his wife, or what someone might have said to coerce her to behave so erratically. Through the years Trevor had become somewhat aware of various tactics used to sway the will and manipulate the mind. He was concerned.

He was deep in thought as he neared the end of the driveway and failed to notice Jeff Johnson in the street until it was too late. Trevor used to call him JJ, but that was years ago, before Jeff made a few observations and remarks about the way Trevor dealt with people. Trevor remained convinced that these went well beyond the point of being neighborly.

"Hello," Jeff said, slowing his Golden Retriever slightly.

Trevor's face soured. "Hey," he said, and then quickly turned away. Jeff moved on.

Trevor left the can by the curb and started walking back up the driveway. His eyes focused momentarily on his home as they so often did from this section of the drive. He enjoyed surveying his property and reminding himself that he had been able to carve out a nice life for he and his wife. Nearing the garage he quickly shifted his thoughts back to the problem at hand.

He entered the house and found his wife in the kitchen gathering up supplies for dinner. The minutes outside had been enough for him to piece together a strategy. He knew enough about human psychology and would need to be careful with his next move, avoiding repellent words like "you can't" and "don't ever." Trevor chose tact over confrontation.

"I thought we were going down to the boat tomorrow," he said.

"I changed my mind," she replied. "Besides, it's too early for that. We could still get snow. You should just leave the cover on for a few more weeks."

Trevor knew too well that April snow was always a possibility in Jersey, but he also knew his will was stronger than his wife's. A bit more force, subtly applied, would surely achieve the desired result.

"I was thinking we could go to Howard's for dinner," he said with a smile, and bumped up against her in a flirtatious manner.

"That sounds nice," she said, taking a step to the side to grab a cutting board that was just out of reach.

*Success.*

"But I promised Beth we could grab some lunch afterwards. Sorry." It was true Cindy had become a stronger woman over the years, much the way hands become calloused under the stress of physical labor, but he couldn't remember a time when she forfeited a date with him for anything.

*Perhaps it's best to just leave things like this. I can spend more time on the boat without her there, maybe get some fishing in. I'm sure she'll see through whatever phony is preaching in the morning, and that lesson will be long remembered. This should turn out to be another win-win situation.*

"Not a problem," he said. "Have a good time, and please say hi to Beth for me." His words were designed to be doubly confusing because not only did Cindy know her husband thought little of church, he also had zero tolerance for Beth.

The unspoken rule for driving in New Jersey is the posted limit, plus ten. Trevor felt no need to break with convention, so his car rolled down Route 287 at about 75 mph. He was feeling pretty good. The morning sun was beaming through the windshield and although the temperature outside was still in the forties, he was toasty warm in the car and it made him think of summer. His *Ocean Drive* CD was in play with *Sloop John B* pumping through the speakers. This was his favorite Beach Boys tune because it was more about sailing and less about surfing. A pair of jelly donuts sat in a bag next to his coffee, and the EZ-Pass gizmo stuck to his windshield guaranteed that he would barely need to slow down before arriving. He still had almost twelve hours before the Sunday evening blues set in, so the nagging realization it would soon be Monday seemed eons away. It was going to be a great trip.

Trevor knew there were only two things that could have made his day better: 30 more degrees on the thermometer and Cindy by his side. It was true he had not always been the best husband—he could admit that to himself—but in the safe place in his mind where he did most of his thinking, there was no one closer to him, no greater ally, no better companion. If she had only received half the attention he lavished on her internally she would never doubt his love. Such was life with this thinker, so many thoughts and so few words. If only she knew.

He noticed his car closing rapidly on the car ahead of him. A quick glance in the mirror, a twist of the wheel, and he passed easily on the left. A few seconds later he drifted back into the middle lane where he felt at home again. As the pavement flew past, Trevor did what he did best—think. After the strange events of the previous day it was important to try and connect the reality he thought existed with the one playing out before his eyes. He needed to understand why Cindy had abandoned reason and common sense.

*What is wrong with her? Is this just a game, or is she serious? Is she just trying to get back at me for something? Perhaps it has to do with the in-laws.*

He had long been at war with his in-laws, but his was not a war fought with strong words and dirty looks, it was far more covert than that. Forgetting to relay a message from mom to daughter was always effective. Making plans to be out of town during a holiday celebration was another weapon in his arsenal. But his personal favorite, the one which drove them all insane, were the *innocent* observations about Cindy's brother and his endless struggle with heroin. These were the words that cut deepest because they highlighted the failure of an entire family, a failure that had taken decades to mature. Trevor knew these words brought pain and embarrassment to his wife, but he always felt a bit of collateral damage could be tolerated since they were so caustic to his mother-in-law.

He crept up on another car and then turned off the cruise control. There was no rhythm to the traffic this morning, so he would be better off without it. He was still troubled by his wife's decision and wondered why she would go against the grain, his grain. He had been and done so much for her, the endless hours he worked to provide for her, the wise decisions that made life better both financially and socially, the constant sacrifice for no one else but her.

*Why wouldn't she trust the judgment of such a good man?*

Trevor was willing to concede that there were times in life when he lost focus, but he could also remember and take pride in many hard battles, fought and won, at a young age. Like so many others who have walked through the pain of a difficult childhood, Trevor had developed a strong personality, and he had grown quite fond of it. He felt it served him well, allowing him to stand against storms in life that would have crushed others. But he also sensed that with each passing year, the armor he adopted early in life was making it harder to stay afloat, like an unrelenting anchor pulling him slowly down below the surface of the water. Usually he pretended not to notice, but sometimes he was far too aware of his condition, arms and legs pumping furiously, trying not to sink. He had never gone under in his younger days. He was equally determined now.

Trevor looked down and noticed his speed had dropped off, lulled to a slower speed by the drivers around him and the thoughts in his mind. He pressed his foot to the accelerator and moved back into the passing lane. Then it hit him, the memory of his father. The ruthless villain in the story of Trevor's life. The selfish, maniacal

11

force that pushed harmony into disarray, paradise into hell. Even at a young age, Trevor had vowed in his heart to be a better man than his father, a much better man. He wondered what might have happened to the man he shared his childhood with, the man he barely knew. But then Trevor quickly hardened, hoping the old man got what he deserved.

He looked down at the gas gauge and chastised himself for not filling up the tank. He hated exiting the highway when he was in the zone, but with more than a quarter tank he decided to keep going, reasonably certain he had enough to make it one way.

His phone rang. He picked it up and saw that it was Bob calling. He debated internally for a second or two and then hit the answer button.

"Hey Bob, what's up?"

"Are you on the road?" Bob asked.

"Absolutely," Trevor said.

"Nice," Bob said. "And how did the review go?"

Trevor turned down the music and let out a groan. "It feels like last year again. Mostly good, but it's the negative stuff that kills me. It overshadows everything. Uncooperative and stubborn were the two words that stuck out the most. I really thought Steve was in my corner. I may have to rethink things a bit."

"He can be two-faced," Bob said. "Just be careful."

"I will," Trevor said. "It just shouldn't be this hard to get a promotion. I feel like I'm running out of allies."

"I know what you mean," Bob said. "I feel like I'm stuck. It's Groundhog Day."

"Phil? Phil Connor? I sure as heck fire remember you," Trevor said and both men let out a laugh.

"Well, just know that I've got your back," Bob said. "But it probably won't do much to help right now."

"I appreciate that," Trevor said. "I've found myself getting pretty disgusted with the place. I feel stuck too, and I don't even like most of the people I work with these days. It's frustrating."

"Just hang in. It'll get better, and you'll have your day in the sun. Until then, enjoy the boat."

"I hope you're right," Trevor said. "Either way, I will enjoy the boat."

"Good. Talk to you later," Bob said.

"Later," Trevor said, and set the phone back down on the passenger seat. He thought for a moment about the people in his life, and how they seemed to fit neatly into two columns, those he loved and those he hated. He wondered if this was a by-product of what his parent's had inadvertently taught him, loving one and hating the other. Whatever its source, Trevor saw little need to shade his feelings from the rest of the world. He seemed unconcerned about how his personal life was affected, but his lack of political correctness was becoming more and more obvious at work and that was a problem. Adding to this dangerous mix was Trevor's decreased interest in his job. He wondered where it might lead. He had enjoyed riding the escalator to the upper tier of the company, but to move forward now he would need more than intelligence and hard work. Now it was about teamwork and cooperation, and he had fought too many hard battles to garner the necessary support to reach the next level. He had become too critical of the individuals that surrounded him and the system under which they thrived, isolating himself from the avenues to power. He knew he was rapidly approaching his professional ceiling and this added fuel to an ever-growing fire.

And then his mind relaxed, accepting that the challenges and turmoil would keep coming, but that Cindy would always be there. Knowing that she understood the trials, and the man who faced them, brought tremendous reassurance.

*But why church? What is she thinking?*

Cindy sat quietly in a church pew, staring at a heavyset man with gentle mannerisms speaking words of conviction and certainty. His eyes bounced from one parishioner to the next, eventually meeting hers. She wondered if the urgency rising up inside of her was born from the strength of the preacher's voice or some intense longing deep within.

For years she had sought fulfillment in her marriage, but never quite found her treasure. She recently became convinced that in Trevor's mind most people were like bit actors in his story, instead of leading men and women in their own. He typically woke before sunrise, hurried through a never-changing 25 minute get ready routine, and then ate his breakfast on the drive to the office. Sometimes he said goodbye to his wife and sometimes he didn't. Some days she heard him mumble something and other days she just slept right through. She never bothered to call him at work anymore because after years of being rushed off the phone, there was no news so important or exciting that it could not wait until he returned home. She filled her days with a part-time job, cleaning, cooking, shopping and decorating. It was a full schedule, a little of this and a little of that, but she always carved some time from each day to wonder if life was supposed to be better than this, if the world she lived in was just a terrible compromise or the best that people in upper-middle class America can hope for.

She had tried on many occasions to talk to Trevor about their relationship. Where it was. Where it had been. Where she wanted it to go. She longed for greater intimacy and a more profound connection. Years ago he listened patiently, but usually offered resistance when she implied they had missed the mark. But as more time passed, his patience waned. The here-we-go-again sighs became more and more pronounced until she barely dared to dream anymore, eventually running out of words to say. She had once thought about the unthinkable, but decided she would remain faithful to her husband, even if it brought about a slow and painful death.

Cindy was in a very hard place. A nauseating emptiness had taken hold of her several months earlier, and nothing she tried could shake it. She had stopped looking for sunsets at the end of each day. It might have driven her to calamity, but she devised a plan, a non-conventional approach for avoiding what she was certain would be a major downfall. Cindy chose four women in her life, based on no particular criteria other than geography, and much like science lab in high school she observed each acquaintance with the hope of discovering what makes for lasting happiness. Somewhere during her four week experiment, Beth was beginning to outshine the others. Call it inner strength, faith, confidence, or whatever the motivational speaker du jour titles his most recent book, there was a distinct difference about her. She could find joy in the good times. She could be patient in the bad times. She could even muster fragments of hope during impossible times. Her tears were real, as were her laughs. She was comfortable enough with her faults and did not feel the need to hide or escape from them. She knew she was flawed, but she also knew there was a great deal more that helped define her, an intricate and rare blend of talent, intelligence, beauty and potential as unique as her fingerprints. Cindy was desperate to know what made her friend this way.

And now she sat beside Beth on a crisp Sunday morning. Slowly, remarkably, something was overtaking her. Like the feeling of coming home after a long and exhausting journey, Cindy felt a peace that could not be easily shaken. This was all so new to her, the sermon, the singing, the unfamiliar crowd, but somehow, more than ever before, she felt safe. She was immersed in joy.

The car rolled down the highway. Trevor had not seen his boat in more than six months and felt like a child on Christmas morning. He slowed just enough to safely follow the curve of the exit, and then quickly sped up as he approached the Parkway. Traffic cones were everywhere due to a new span being added to the Driscoll Bridge. Trevor took his eyes off the road to study the unfinished concrete and rebar to his right, and then it happened.

The bus driver had been this way more than a hundred times. He knew every turn along the Parkway from Essex County to Atlantic City, but the cones had been moved two days earlier altering

16

the traffic patterns approaching the bridge. It might have made more sense to drive cautiously, especially when fifty lives hang in the balance, but young men often consider themselves invincible. After plowing down more than a dozen cones and drifting dangerously close to a mini-van, the driver over corrected his vehicle and found himself darting into the lane on his right. The thud was barely noticeable to most on the bus, but it was enough to right the large vehicle. Unfortunately there are two sides to every collision.

Trevor's car was rocked by the bus and his head slammed hard against the window. The pain was instantaneous and the haze it cast over his consciousness lasted for seconds. The unexpected jolt set his car on a new course toward the unfinished addition of the bridge. Even this he might have recovered from, but the much larger bus transferred some of its momentum to the car as well. The images and sounds that registered with Trevor seemed anything but real. The surprisingly loud sound of wheels slapping over loose sheets of plywood. Cones flashing by at frightening speed. The ominous screech of rebar tearing at the body of his car, followed by the emptiness and dread of near silence.

As the car traveled the more than one hundred feet between the road surface and the Raritan River, there was enough time for Trevor to stop panicking and evaluate his situation. His stomach winced as the car rocked forward. If only the front of the car would hit water first, he might draw some benefit from the airbag. He wanted the impact sooner than later, and heard himself utter two words that felt strange moving across his lips.

"Please God."

Convinced he could survive the collision, his mind raced to establish a plan of escape for the moment his car sunk into the frigid river. He tried to recall and assemble every safety tip he had learned over the course of a lifetime into a single coherent plan when—crash! The blow was softened by the airbag, but was bone crushing all the same. This was the second major impact he had felt in the span of seconds and all focus seemed to escape him once again. His world became a blur of white nylon, shattered glass, and frigid water. He knew he was alive, yet at that moment his mind seemed incapable of processing any additional information. Trevor was in a fight for his life, but his brain was faltering.

Water continued rushing into the vehicle and Trevor could feel the sting on his legs. He lost discernment between up and down, left and right. Everything was happening too fast and his thoughts could not keep up. He strained to free himself, but was unable to move from his seat. Cold water rushed over his stomach causing him to remember the seatbelt. He groped for the release but his hands were still disconnected from his thinking. Where was it?

Trevor's chest was now submerged. He had only a few seconds left. He would need one deep breath before the car went completely under if he were to have any chance. Maybe it was the chilly water, or perhaps the intense adrenaline rush, either way, his mind was clearing. His survival instincts were returning and he was ready to fight again. Three. Two. One. He drew in as much air as he could, but something felt terribly wrong. There was a strange pressure on his chest, as if someone placed a 200 pound weight there. His count had failed him and he took in far more water than air. He panicked, flailing his arms in a haphazard manner. Meanwhile, his chest convulsed a number of times involuntarily, seeking the air it desperately needed. Then it stopped. Trevor no longer struggled. With the battle now lost his mind calmed to the inevitable. Time slowed to a crawl. He thought momentarily about his wife and then all faded to black.

# 2

# The Beginning of the In-Between

It was dark but Trevor felt warm. As if waking from a dream, he had no idea where he was. The first thing he realized was that he was standing. He slid his hand over his pants and noticed they were dry. He then experimented with his leg to see if it would move. It did. He set it in front of him about six inches, one small step for man. He took another step, slowly and carefully, so as not to put himself in danger. He continued cautiously through the darkness with his hands held slightly ahead of him to avoid collisions. There were not many times in life his eyes sensed a complete absence of light and it left him feeling weak and vulnerable.

Based on the contour of the ground below his feet he quickly concluded that he was not in a building, but there were too many unknowns for his mind to deal with. He wanted to collapse, or at least drop down on all fours so he could move safely. Still he kept on, not fully understanding why, but without many options. It could have been his imagination, or the slow adjustment of human eyes to a dimly lit space, but there seemed to be a trace of light growing around him. This led to another discovery: he was walking through a narrow cave. There was more light ahead.

His pace improved slightly as he gained a better view of the cave floor. He felt close to normal now. His legs were strong, his breathing relaxed. A strange calm settled over him. The entrance to the cave was now only about 20 yards away and the light pouring in was strong and bright. He was curious.

Trevor stepped out from the cave, immediately lost in the view before him, no longer certain he was still breathing. He could feel the sun on his shoulders and a slight breeze blowing through his hair, but found it nearly impossible to pull his eyes away from that sculpture of rock and earth reaching out in all directions. Whether he was standing near the peak of a single mountain, or close to the ridge of an entire range, he could not say for sure. Trevor was, at the very least, a couple of thousand feet above the valley below. The diminishing elevations, rolling down from his perch, formed a mighty staircase ending in a large expanse of flatlands. The valley then continued for what must have been tens of miles until it rested again at the foot of another mountain range. The greens, browns, grays and blues were as clear and rich as any he could remember. He finally drew a deep breath.

*Maybe this is heaven.*

He quickly laughed at his foolishness when the patterns etched deeply into his brain took charge once again.

*There is no heaven.*

It seemed strange that the conclusion which had brought so much comfort in the past did little to help him now.

*What is this place?*

His head remained motionless as his eyes scanned the valley, identifying details that typically would have escaped him. A few heartbeats later he found himself manufacturing an answer to his most pressing question as the internal monologue began.

*This is remarkable. Somehow I must still be alive. My body must be fighting for survival. The shock to my system and the damage to my body have pushed my consciousness into this paradise, to keep it from getting in the way of healing. The pain must have been too great. How extraordinary, to think that our minds and bodies have evolved to such an extent, and adapted such a skill.*

With a sound conclusion in place he relaxed, knowing his body was working hard to repair the damage wrought by the accident. Yes, he remembered the accident. He knew the best thing he could do right now was to enjoy his dream, each and every aspect it presented. There would be time for struggle later. Time to deal with the pains of a broken body. Time to put his shattered life back in order. For now he was in a better place.

He was glad it was Spring, or at the latest early Summer. The fresh growth and warmth created an inviting environment; he could even smell new life in the air. He took a few steps to his left and kicked a small rock that got in his way. It rolled for a few feet before bouncing off the trunk of a pine tree. He lifted his hand to touch the needles on a nearby branch.

*It seems so real.*

He felt a trace of sap on his fingers and rubbed them against his thumb to remove the sticky goo. He wanted to laugh. His mind's attention to detail was staggering.

"It's not a dream," a voice spoke. Trevor's head snapped to the right and his first reaction was fear. He did not expect anyone and had failed to notice the young man just a few yards away.

"What?" Trevor asked. He wanted to say more, to pry, to

intimidate, but found himself caught completely off guard. One simple question was all his mind could produce.

"It's all real, everything you see before you. The sounds, the smells, the tastes. It's not a dream, in case that's what you were thinking." The young man spoke slowly and deliberately.

Trevor continued studying the man. He had to be older than 20, but 30 would have been a stretch. He wasn't very tall or good looking, in fact, there wasn't one eye-catching feature about him. He was mediocre in all respects. His blond hair was buzzed nearly down to his scalp, much like a cadet during basic training, but the scruff around his mouth and jaw betrayed that image. There were a number of scars visible on his forehead and his ears looked a few sizes too large for his skull. Still, he did appear extremely confident, and not just the shallow cockiness of a young rebel with a few too many beers in him. His was more the quiet confidence of a man who fully understands and appreciates his place in life and the land on which he lives.

Trevor's Darwinian instincts surfaced as they so often did in the company of a rival male, and doing what he did best, he began taking inventory. Although considerably older, he had almost six inches on the younger man and much more meat on his bones. Trevor was confident this meant greater strength, which would be important if there was any kind of trouble. Trevor's extra years or decades equated to greater wisdom, that was pretty much a given. Down the list he went, comparing the things he could see, as well as those he imagined. When Trevor was done a few seconds later, convinced that he was the alpha presence, he felt ready to engage the stranger.

"Where am I?" Trevor asked.

The young man smiled. He had been holding a backpack in his right hand and set it down on the ground next to another just like it. He walked over to Trevor in a slow and relaxed manner, holding out his hand in friendship. "I'm Zachary," he said, "but Zac is a lot easier on the tongue and makes me feel a lot less formal."

"Trevor," came the reply. He often kept his words short in situations like this.

"We call it the In-Between," Zac said. "You can probably guess why."

Trevor looked back over the valley and nodded his head as if to indicate it was all understood, but hardly any of it was. There were still too many things that didn't make sense. There was also a twinge of regret. Trevor had always enjoyed solitude in the presence of mountains and oceans. Today was no different. He wrestled with the idea of having someone else here, wondered if Zac might be a useful companion in a place as unfamiliar as this, but then quickly decided it was too early to draw such positive judgments.

"Do you have any questions?" Zac asked.

Trevor's mind was full of questions, much like it had always been, but only one demanded an answer. "How did I get here?" he asked timidly, somewhat fearful of the response, but still not convinced this was more than a dream.

"Do you remember anything?" Zac asked.

Trevor nodded, and as he did images of the struggle filled his head. The accident. The fall. The river.

"I'm sorry," Zac said, "it wasn't an easy ending."

"Are you saying—" Trevor started, but then stopped himself mid-sentence. He was baffled, as if two plus two failed to equal four. Zac stood quiet for a few seconds, knowing that too many words now would only make things worse, but too few could be just as dangerous.

"Can I help?" Zac asked.

Trevor, feeling sick to his stomach, tipped his head to say yes, but couldn't bring words to his mouth. Zac took two steps back, knowing the extra distance would help someone of Trevor's makeup. He looked into Trevor's eyes and began.

"Your life on earth ended in the river this morning. Over there, that ridgeline in the distance, that's where eternity begins. Between here and there lies the In-Between. I'm here to guide you to the other side."

Trevor put his hand on his stomach. He wanted to puke. How could life be over? He still had so much to accomplish–so much to experience. He had never seen Yosemite, Alaska, or the Bay of Fundy. He never started writing his book, playing the guitar, hiking the Appalachian Trail or pushing the pedal to the floor in a '57 Chevy. The boat he purchased just last year, his ticket to fun and adventure, had barely made it beyond the inlet. There would be no skiing in the Alps or kayaking in the fjords of Norway. He had always wanted to start his own business, or at the very least spend a few years as a consultant. And what about all that time with Cindy they had talked about when they were younger and deeper in love? Where did it all go? How could it be over?

Trevor looked out across the valley and tears welled in his eyes. In forty some odd years of life he had never been more despondent, even when his mom died back in '03. He felt the crushing weight of failure and missed opportunities pressing hard upon his shoulders. Suddenly, so much of what seemed important yesterday was replaced with regret, deep regret, the kind that seeps into the marrow of a hurting soul. He had spent six years in college and then countless hours at the job. Now he felt stupid and small. He could have spent time with his wife, time with friends, or even with his family. He could have built relationships to savor, something to carry with him beyond the gates of death. But now he was completely alone and the weight of that reality was crushing him. He had been such a fool.

He thought in that instant about how much money he would trade for another week, another day, or even another hour with his beautiful bride. He would gladly forfeit every ounce of his wealth just to share a few more words with her, words to right a marriage that was always less than it should have been. Words to put his wife at ease, to allow her to finally realize how much she meant to him. It seemed odd that money, prestige, and motor boats could mean so much to a man during one moment, and so little the next. So many times he heard the old adage about never knowing when it will be over, but now that lesson was painfully real. Still there was more to come.

Along with the regret of missed relationships and wasted time came anguish from recognizing all the pain he had brought to others. There were the kids in grade school he laughed at and tormented. Having an abusive father no longer seemed like a valid excuse for such behavior. There were the girls he took advantage of on dates. The people he ruthlessly manipulated and undermined at work. The neighbor whom he dismissed as unworthy of friendship or even the slightest courtesy. There were so many, too many, most of whom he had forgotten or ignored until now, those he mocked and those he belittled. Words that dealt pain, his words, kept ringing in his ears as faces full of hurt and sorrow kept scrolling through his thoughts. But mostly, and most importantly, there was Cindy, the wife he never completely shared his life with. He could see her face, timid, uncertain and disappointed, perhaps wondering why there was distance between them.

Trevor wanted to cry. The pain inside was overtaking him and while caught up in this overwhelming sadness he failed to notice that Zac was standing close to him again. The young man reached out his hand and placed it on Trevor's shoulder. Without knowing why, Trevor leaned in and placed his head on the stranger's shoulder. Zac seemed much larger now, and as he wrapped his arms around Trevor, the broken man wept bitterly. Zac's tears mixed with Trevor's as if the pain were his own.

Somewhere, in the midst of all this suffering and regret something wonderful began happening. Trevor, for the first time since he had been stained by the ugliness of life, felt relief. The wrongs he had done, the wrongs that had been done to him, were fading. Trevor found release. The pain was leaving him. It felt good. It felt different. It felt raw, and new, and untamed. Eventually he found the strength to step back from the younger man. It was then that he noticed that Zac had been crying with him.

*What kind of man is this?*

"It is finished," Zac said, "those days are behind you now."

Trevor could feel the weight being lifted from him. As quickly as pain and shame took hold of him, he found himself released from its grip. His mind was still ripe with memories, but the regret was gone. Images of Cindy fired in his head: working in the garden, jumping into a wave, and relaxing in the hammock. Others of childhood friends and laughter on the job came into focus as well. There were no tears, no sadness, only joy and happiness. He would carry just the good from this point forward. The jealousy and anger had been left in a distant land and a forgotten time. It was hard to comprehend. It was unworldly.

"I guess I had a few things mixed up," Trevor admitted.

"A few," Zac agreed. "Welcome to the human race."

Trevor smiled. Had he known that forgiveness could make such a remarkable impact he might have asked for it decades ago. He might have offered it to others as well.

"So what now?" Trevor asked, wiping tears from his cheek.

"Like I said," Zac started, "we need to get to the other side of the valley. It's going to take a few days but we have plenty of food in our packs."

"And what then?" Trevor asked.

"I guess that's up to you," Zac said, "but we have a lot of distance to cover before sunset, so we should probably be on our way." Zac picked up a backpack and handed it to Trevor, who then placed it on his shoulders. Zac spent a minute adjusting the straps so the pack remained high and comfortable.

"How is that?" Zac asked.

Trevor raised and lowered his shoulders a few times as a quick test. "Feels pretty good," he said. Unsure if he should ask his next question, he kept silent for a few seconds, but felt it might scorch his tongue if he failed to spit it out.

"Is this heaven?"

Zac finished adjusting the straps of his own pack and then looked at Trevor with a grin.

"Do you believe in heaven?"

Trevor had been caught and they both knew it. A smirk or frown formed on his lips, he wasn't sure which.

"No, I guess I don't," Trevor said.

"That's what I thought," Zac said. "Come on, we're burning daylight."

With that, the two men started down the mountain. Trevor always liked that line about burning daylight and appreciated the tribute to the Duke. He wasn't sure if Zac knew more than he let on or just assumed every male of his era was a John Wayne fan. Maybe it didn't matter. Maybe nothing mattered anymore.

And as quickly as that, Trevor left the only world he had ever known, forever. It never occurred to him to ask if he could return, or even look back. That is how things play out in the In-Between, breaking the grip of the world and preparing for eternity.

# 3
## The Descent

The two men worked their way down a narrow path, Zac in front and Trevor not far behind. Years had passed since Trevor's last mountain hike and now he wondered why that was. He loved being outdoors, but like so many other pleasures in life, Trevor had let them slip away in exchange for something less.

Trevor could already tell that this was a special place. The mountains were soft and green, much like the Appalachians he enjoyed as a young man. The majority of his college days had been spent at James Madison University and periodically he carved out sizable chunks of time to head off into the mountains, sometimes with a friend, but usually on his own. It did him good then, allowing him to reconnect and center himself. It was doing him good now.

Neither man spoke for quite some time. Zac, convinced that the surroundings were having a profound impact on Trevor, felt no need to communicate. Trevor, needing time to process all that was happening, failed to notice the silence. And so they continued, sometimes uphill, often down, moving slowly toward the valley floor.

"How about a break?" Zac eventually offered while sitting down upon a large rock just off the trail.

"Really?" Trevor asked, somewhat surprised. "Why don't we just keep going? I'm fine." He was used to struggling, working harder than most in every situation that presented itself. It was his edge, the secret weapon that brought him success when others faltered. It started in high school, maintaining a high GPA and running cross country. He had even made third team All County. Then in college it was study and work, study and work. He left a little time to party, because after all, it was college, but there were few on campus that pressed harder than Trevor. After graduation there were long hours at work, projects at home, and sometimes when he needed a breather he set off on a long run. He lived his life like a workhorse, always driven to do and accomplish more. To stop and take a break after barely more than an hour of hiking seemed strange to him.

"Is that all you want, to be fine?" Zac asked. "Or would you like to be good, maybe even great? If you had your choice, what would you choose?"

"We don't often get to choose in life, do we?" Trevor countered. He was proud of his words, proud that he offered a good defense to his position, but inside, in a vulnerable place that Trevor could barely acknowledge, he didn't know if he agreed with it any longer. Life had been hard, that was true, but maybe he had made it harder than it needed to be. He was realizing that now, but wasn't about to forfeit a *discussion* over something as trivial as self doubt or internal reflection. All regret was gone, but Trevor's survival skills were very much intact, and although Zac posed no threat to him, Trevor still preferred to walk a well worn path carved in an earlier life.

"I'm not sure," Zac said in a soft voice, "but I think maybe we do."

Trevor was torn. He knew how to win a debate, but at this moment he found himself wishing he knew how to lose one. He wanted to give up, thinking maybe there was something he could learn from the younger man, but something inside kept driving him forward to a place he had been so many times before. A place he no longer wanted to go.

"It's probably not that important," Zac said, disarming Trevor in an instant. "I just find that if I'm always busy hiking, there are many things I miss along the way. So if it's okay with you, can we take a break now and then?"

"That sounds fair," Trevor said, willing to offer up some honesty. "I think I am better than most at missing things along the way."

"Yeah," Zac agreed with a smile on his face, "I think you may be right."

They shared a laugh, and then each man pulled a water jug from the side of their pack and subdued a thirst before it had a chance to mature. Trevor considered the wisdom of this, meeting a need before it became an urgency. Preventing fires before they began. He thought about this in the context of his life, and how many times he found himself a slave to the urgent. It seemed odd to him how he once believed he had everything figured out. Now he could recognize how he missed much that should have been obvious, things that even a child should know.

Trevor eventually noticed they had stopped near an overlook. Although not quite the eagle's perspective he had seen when he first exited the cave, the view into the valley was stunning. He was now closer to the valley and could appreciate its size, but there was still only a finite distance separating him from eternity. He found that quite intimidating.

As his eyes roamed the landscape he began to pick up details he had missed up to this point. There were countless trees in the valley, and in most cases they were grouped together in thick forests. It might have been a single forest at one time, but soft green and brown patches had been carved randomly throughout. He slowly realized those clearings were farmland. Looking closer he could make out a number of farm-houses. He imagined each being home to a family, and it brought relief to think that he was not the only person in this land. Trevor certainly enjoyed time on his own more than most, but he also knew that complete solitude could be a sentence that was too hard to bear.

He noticed a river cutting its way through the landscape with gentle turns, convincing Trevor it had been there for a very long time. It was guarded on either side by a thin band of trees, and every so often it was fed by a smaller stream and grew in width as it moved through the valley. There was a thin brown line, most likely a dirt road, leading into what looked to be a small village. He spied a faint dust cloud rising from the road.

*Could it be? People? Where are they from? How long have they been there?*

He considered how each person down in the valley must be on a journey—a journey much like his. Each had a story to tell of footsteps left behind, an end which really wasn't, and an unknown still ahead. Trevor wanted to know more. He wanted to be with and talk to the others. He wanted to recount his story, and have stories told to him. He wanted to share his life, or whatever this was, with anyone and everyone he could find. This was out of character for Trevor, but the strangeness or newness of this land was pushing him in a new direction.

When it was time to move on, the two men followed the path through a gathering of trees which quickly faded away. Zac stopped and turned to Trevor.

"The next piece is a little tricky, but I think you'll do fine." Trevor, looking past Zac, could see the face of a cliff that was not quite vertical, but still very dangerous. He stepped to one side to get a better view and estimated the cliff to be at least two or three hundred feet in height. The path, no more than a couple of feet in width, traversed the face of the cliff. It unnerved him.

"Is there another way?" Trevor asked.

"Yes, but it would take us way out of the way," Zac said.

Zac set out first, sliding his right hand along the cliff face for balance. He looked relaxed and confident. Trevor followed, much slower and more carefully. The path rose slightly at first and then sloped downward at a steeper angle, growing narrower in places. The footing was solid but rough, and Trevor could feel his heart racing. The further he walked, the slower his steps became. Eventually he turned his body sideways, leaning strongly into the cliff with both hands, his face pressed against rock. He slid his left foot to the side, and then followed with his right. He kept this up for a number of steps and then stopped, a victim to fear, frozen on a ledge barely more than a foot wide.

Zac was now standing on the far side of the cliff. "Are you okay?" he called out.

"I need a minute," Trevor said in a deflated tone. His hands gripped tightly to rock, refusing to let go, and his neck was hunched as if under a burden.

Zac moved back onto the face of the cliff and made his way to Trevor. He turned sideways, just like Trevor, with both hands against the cliff.

"Grab my arm," Zac said.

"I don't think I can," Trevor said.

"Can't or won't?" Zac asked.

"What difference does it make?" Trevor said. He felt weak and embarrassed.

"Listen, I want you to let go of what you think is solid."

"We could both fall," Trevor said.

"It's time you learned to trust someone other than yourself," Zac said. "Just grab my arm."

Trevor slowly pulled his left hand off the wall and reached for Zac's arm. Once found, he grabbed as much shirt as his hand would allow, and held tightly. Trevor noticed immediately that his body was calming.

"We'll do this together," Zac said, taking a short step to the side with his left foot. "Left," he said. Trevor followed his lead. Zac then slid his right foot toward his left. "Now right." Slowly and methodically the two men made their way along the ledge. Trevor held on for life, impressed by the strength in Zac's arm and the certainty of his step.

35

When they finally made it to safer ground, Zac patted Trevor on the back. "Good job. I told you that wasn't an easy stretch."

Trevor, emotionally fatigued, sat down on a large rock. "I don't know what's wrong with me," he said apologetically.

"Stop," Zac said, "It took a great deal of courage to cross that span. You handled it well. And you even learned a little about trusting someone else. I would say you have nothing to be ashamed of." Zac then turned and was moving again.

Trevor wasn't quite ready to follow; he needed time to recharge. He watched Zac disappear into another patch of trees and wondered why anyone would risk their life for someone they barely knew. It seemed strange to Trevor. He took a few deep breaths and then was on his way.

They kept up throughout the morning, taking occasional breaks at Zac's discretion to look out over the valley or study some unique rock or plant, but Trevor was the one to instigate lunch. They took time to enjoy a sandwich, observe squirrels at work in a nearby tree, and talk about more of the things Trevor spent a lifetime avoiding.

Trevor eventually looked to Zac and asked, "Does anyone ever get it right? Life, I mean."

Zac looked away toward the valley somewhat lost in thought, and just as Trevor started feeling awkward about being ignored, Zac slowly nodded his head. "Yeah, there are a few. But for most it's like driving from one side of a continent to the other without a map. You can imagine how many chances there are to lose your way."

"Why is it so hard?" Trevor asked. "Why does it have to be

that way?"

"It doesn't have to be," Zac responded. "People just make bad choices. They want too much, give too little, and usually settle for far less than they should. Back to my question, if you could choose to live a great life or just a mediocre one, which would you choose?"

"I think I'd want great," Trevor replied.

"Really?" Zac questioned.

Trevor threw up his hands in self-defense. "I didn't know any better." He paused for a moment knowing he had more to say. His voice softened. "I probably wouldn't have listened anyway." It wasn't an easy concession, but he felt good about making it.

"Probably not," Zac agreed. "And such is the human condition. Give me free will, let me decide, but when things go wrong, let me blame someone, anyone, other than myself. You're not alone. History is filled with people just like you. That's why there had to be another way."

"Another way?" Trevor asked.

"Sorry," Zac said. "I'm getting ahead of myself. We'll have plenty of time to talk about that later. We should get going, we still have a lot of ground to cover."

With that the two readied their packs and were on their way. In another life, given a response such as this, Trevor would have hounded and persisted until he was in the know. But in this life, with this companion, he felt it was best to wait. He knew instinctively that when Zac felt it was time for him to know, he would know. He was also trying to remain on his best behavior, feeling like an uninvited guest in a land where he did not belong. He kept his mouth shut and his feet moving. He knew things might change later, but for now, quiet obedience seemed like his best option.

Trevor sensed his mind was downshifting, pacing itself for a more relaxed existence. He didn't need to process thought at breakneck speeds anymore as there were no more self-imposed deadlines or schedules. It was actually hard to remember the last time he felt zero pressure to get something done.

*Who else would try to launch their boat in April?*

His life had been driven by a relentless master bent on squeezing every ounce of life from his being without offering any real hope or peace. Now he was released from that burden.

At some point in the late afternoon Trevor sensed his legs had grown noticeably weaker. It suddenly became clear that he was still operating in a 44 year old, earth-born body that had gone too many years without a decent maintenance plan. This brought to mind a number of other questions he had been juggling throughout the day, and with increased confidence in the relationship between he and Zac, he decided it was time to speak up.

"Can I pick your brain a little?" he asked.

Zac laughed lightly and said, "I can't believe you waited this long. Go ahead."

The words put Trevor more at ease, and he spent a few quiet moments composing his thoughts. Looking carefully at his hand he asked, "It still looks and feels like me. Is it?"

"The short answer is yes", Zac began, "but the long answer is far more interesting. What'll it be?"

"Long answer for 800, Alex!" Trevor said.

"Okay then," Zac replied. "Just keep in mind you may not be quite ready to hear all of this. First things first. Death, like the one you experienced in the other world, is not an end, it is just another beginning. And this journey, the one you are on now, has an end as well, but that end is the beginning of the never-ending."

"Do you always talk in riddles?" Trevor asked.

"No, not always," Zac said. "Your death brought you out of the old world and into the next, but it was like passing through a filter. Into this world you brought your mind, your body, memories, dreams, personality, but some things were left behind. The pain, the regret, the judgment and condemnation, the ghosts that torment and destroy, those are all things that would keep you from making a fresh start. We don't need them here. They would only get in the way. This world, this dimension—whatever you want to call it—should be short lived, days instead of years. I'm here as your guide, and as I said before, I will be with you until you get to where you need to be. Once there, you will be offered a choice."

"Great," Trevor interrupted in a sarcastic tone, "I've done a real good job with choices so far."

"Funny thing about that," Zac continued, "those who really understand how things work know that the past is no reliable indicator of the future, so again, don't be so hard on yourself. And don't be surprised to find yourself a very different person on the other side of this valley. Anyway, the path is going to fork before it heads off into those mountains. You will need to choose one way or the other, and that will be the road to take you home."

"But how will I know which path takes me home?" Trevor

questioned.

"Yes," Zac answered, grinning from ear to ear. "All I can say now is that somehow you will know. I haven't asked much of you, but I am asking for your trust. Are you okay with that?"

Trevor nodded, not entirely sure why. He was still reasonably certain he had the ability to mess things up, only this time for eternity. It remained a serious concern for him, but at that moment Zac turned off the trail and to his left.

"Come on, I want to show you something," Zac said.

Trevor followed along a path of stone that dead ended on a narrow rock outcropping. Zac worked his way near the edge, but Trevor stayed a few steps back. The wind, funneled by the surrounding terrain, was strong here, and blew across their faces and through their hair. They stared at the mountains on the far side of the valley. The sun sat not far above the peaks, slowly approaching them.

"That's quite a view," Trevor said.

"No," Zac said, "I brought you out here because I wanted you to feel something you couldn't see."

Trevor turned to Zac, unclear about what he was saying, or what was meant by it. Zac closed his eyes and drew a deep breath. He lifted his arms away from his body, like a bird preparing for flight. His hands opened wide, and Trevor could see the tiny hairs on those hands swept back and forth by the wind. Suddenly, without saying another word, Zac turned and walked back toward the trail. Trevor looked out toward the valley once more as a final gust brushed against his face, and then he followed Zac.

Not long afterward, Zac pointed out a small inn at the foot of the mountain and the conversation shifted to dinner. They were now less than half a mile away and Trevor realized how easily his hard earned hunger could monopolize his thoughts. He was glad to be near the end of the descent. His thighs were sore and his feet had paid a high price for the miles behind, but more than this he felt a burning curiosity about the valley before him and the days ahead.

# 4

## Disloyalty

The inn looked like a place lumberjacks might frequent. With massive logs forming the walls and only a small number of windows, it seemed out of place in the twenty-first century. Trevor could hear the murmur of a crowd inside and wasn't quite sure what to expect, but the warm light pouring through the windows and the smell of food made it irresistible. Zac opened the door and both men stepped inside. There were a couple dozen tables positioned throughout the room, almost all with guests. A large bar surrounded by stools curved around part of the room, and everyone in the place seemed to have a beer in their hand. There was no music, which seemed odd to Trevor, but there was plenty of noise. As soon as the door shut behind them every eye in the place turned in their direction and the room became unnaturally silent.

"Are you sure about this?" Trevor asked quietly.

"It'll be fine," Zac said. "Have a seat at the bar. I want to see if they have any rooms left. Here, give me your pack."

Zac grabbed the other backpack and walked from the main room into an adjacent hallway. Trevor made his way to the bar. There were only a couple of empty stools and he didn't feel right about sitting next to an attractive woman, so he grabbed a seat between a crusty old-timer and a mountain sized man wearing a thick flannel shirt. He sat there uncomfortably for a couple of minutes without speaking or being spoken to. Finally the bartender approached.

"What'll it be?" the bartender asked.

"I don't have any money," Trevor said. "At least I don't think I do." He checked his pockets but came up empty.

"Give him a beer on me," said the big man.

"No, you don't have to do that," Trevor protested.

The old man, sensing trouble, interceded. "You ought not turn down a beer from Dylan, mister. By the way, I'm Chester, Chester Allan Butterfield."

"I'm Trevor," he said, shaking the old man's hand. Trevor turned back slowly toward Dylan and attempted some damage control. "Sorry about that. We've been walking all day, and, uh, I just wasn't thinking straight."

Dylan nodded, just once, and then motioned to the bartender. "You with that other guy?" he asked in an unfriendly tone.

"Yes," Trevor said, "we're heading across the valley."

"That's what I thought," Dylan said.

The bartender set a beer in front of Trevor and walked away. The first sip was an experiment and proved the beer would have been worth paying for. Maybe it was because he drank nothing but water for the entire day, maybe it was because he was thirsty and tired, either way, his second sip went much deeper into the glass.

Trevor glanced for a few seconds in Dylan's direction, not sure what to say or do. Feeling somewhat uncomfortable, he looked down at his glass until the silence was broken.

"You trust that guy, do ya'?" Dylan asked point blank.

Trevor shrugged his shoulders. "What choice do I have?" It was a stupid answer to a stupid question. Zac had shown more character and compassion in one day than most of Trevor's friends had in a lifetime. But Trevor was still well versed in cheap clichés and pointless banter, so the response rolled off his tongue before any real thought had a chance to congeal.

"Do you always sound so stupid?" Dylan asked before taking a large swallow.

"I guess what I meant is that he's in charge. He found me in the mountains and led the way here. I hadn't seen anyone else 'til I got here, so I just assumed I should do what he says."

"You're not helping your case," Dylan said. "Still sounds pretty stupid to me."

Trevor looked back toward Chester with confusion. "Am I missing something here?" Trevor asked. "I don't really know what is going on. If you guys have any information I should know about, I could really use the help."

"Just be careful," Dylan said. "There are a lot of stories floating around about that guy."

"What kind of stories?" Trevor asked. He was genuinely concerned. Eight or more hours of time spent together were now put into question by three minutes and a beer.

"Look," Dylan said, "he comes through here all the time, and he's always crossing the valley with someone as green as you. He always comes back this way, but always by himself. Seems a bit odd, don't you think?"

"But there's a reason for that, right?" Trevor stopped paying attention to his beer and stared at the big man.

Dylan chuckled. "Let me guess, the fork in the road at the far side of the valley?"

Trevor's eyes scanned the floor. He felt betrayed. He could see that this place wasn't all that different from the world he had left behind. Zac's words all sounded so inviting, but now Trevor wondered if it was just an elaborate hoax designed to hide a much darker truth. He looked back toward Dylan.

"Listen, I need your help," Trevor pleaded. "If you know something that I don't, you need to tell me." For the first time since arriving in the In-Between Trevor felt his judgment had sorely failed him. He was realizing just how little he knew about Zac and his mind succumbed to the weight of doubt. Part of him wished that feelings such as these could have been left behind as well, but maybe they came across for protection and self-preservation.

"We don't really even know the guy," Dylan spoke, "we just hear stories. Lots and lots of stories." Dylan laughed a little harder and this time the old man joined in.

Trevor reached out his hand and grabbed the big man by the arm, only to pull it back quickly when Dylan's glare made it clear that Trevor was overstepping his bounds.

"Could you please give me a clue about what is going on here?" Trevor begged.

"I don't know," Dylan responded coldly with a sinister grin on his face. "I don't want to talk bad about your friend."

"He's not my friend," Trevor protested. "He's just some guy I met this morning. I don't know anything about him. For all I know

45

he's just some lunatic that prowls the mountains looking for people like me."

"They had one room left," Zac said. He was standing right behind Trevor and it was obvious to everyone nearby that Zac heard things he was never meant to hear.

Trevor looked back in horror. He felt like a fool. There were many times in his old life when he said things he shouldn't have and didn't really care, but these were words he deeply regretted. He could tell from the corner of his eye that Dylan was loving every second of this. There was nothing Trevor could say except, "I am so sorry."

"It's okay Trevor," Zac said, "I forgive you." The words were spoken with such sincerity they actually made Trevor feel less guilty. Zac then lightly grabbed Trevor's hair and gently shook his head in short strokes from side to side. "I'll be over there when you're done," he said, pointing to the other side of the room.

And as quick as that, Zac turned and walked toward an empty table. Trevor was bewildered. Instant and complete forgiveness was such an alien concept in Trevor's world that it jarred his mind. Along with that, the head shake catapulted Trevor decades into his past. It was a summer afternoon at Mountain Lake, and one of the few great days he spent with his father. Bored with fishing, young Trevor leapt from the dock and started swimming. He was well beyond the middle of the lake before his dad waved him back in. The boy's adventurous spirit must have tickled the older fisherman, because as Trevor climbed back onto the dock he felt a hand grab the short hair on top of his head, shaking it playfully and lovingly. That was the last good memory Trevor held of his father, and it had escaped him for decades, until now.

Trevor said a quick goodbye to Dylan and the old man, listened reluctantly to a few quick nuggets of *wisdom*, and then made his way to the table. He felt small. He had betrayed a loyal companion for the price of a beer and there was nothing he could do now to have it undone. Perhaps another apology would appease Zac, or maybe he could pretend that he felt physically threatened by the big man and just wanted to go along with anything he said. There had to be some way out of this. Shame had taken over and Trevor was reaching back for all the skills he relied on in a previous life, the same skills that stunted and destroyed relationships.

As Trevor pulled a chair from the table, the words were already flowing. "I really need to apologize for that."

"It must be hard for you to understand forgiveness," Zac said with his attention focused more on a wrinkled, one-page menu than on Trevor. "Why do you think that is?"

"I screwed up," Trevor said. He was in a groveling mood. He didn't want to lose Zac's help or his companionship. "You've been nothing but kind to me, and I shouldn't have said that. I just got really scared and stupid."

"I meant what I said."

"About what?" Trevor asked.

Zac put down the menu, leaned forward, and stared into Trevor's eyes. "I forgive you. If you feel you need to ask me five hundred times to somehow earn my forgiveness, that is your call, but it's four hundred and ninety-nine times more than you need to. Sure, I wish you hadn't said those things, but doesn't everyone make mistakes? Isn't everyone weak, or foolish, or thoughtless at one time or another? Forgiveness is like air. We all need it, and we need it desperately. How can I fault you for needing air? You're forgiven. Now, can we please order? I'm starving." A warm smile formed on Zac's face.

Trevor stared hard at Zac, certain he looked older and wiser than his years. He picked up his menu, shaking a bit, still without a full understanding of what was happening. How could this be? Forgiveness? No second thoughts, bitterness, or grudges? He wanted to talk this out. He had many questions and much to learn. Inside, however, in the hidden compartments that still carried the stain of the old world, he didn't feel he had the right.

It was also hard for Trevor to admit that he was wrong. Not for the insulting words he had spoken—he had no problem apologizing for that—it was hard to admit that the unforgiveness he had shown others throughout his first life had been unjustifiable and selfish, nothing more than one guilty man pronouncing harsh sentence upon another. Trevor looked back and could see that each judgment denying forgiveness became a single brick in an ever growing wall. And as it grew, the wall became more imposing and harder to bring down. After years and decades, the wall stood so massive that tearing it down would have crushed the man who built it, or so he thought. What Trevor failed to realize earlier was that the wall he built to separate himself from those less desirable had actually become more like a prison than a fortress, isolating him from those around him. It prevented him from reaching most of his potential, causing him to remain shallow and underdeveloped. He realized now that if he could have brought the wall down, he might have tasted something far more satisfying.

Trevor wondered if he was so stubborn and set in his ways that he would now start building a second life filled with the same regrets as in the previous one? Would he forever make those same mistakes?

"You seem pretty quiet," Zac said when their meal hit the table. "Anything you want to talk about?"

Trevor let out a sigh. He was struggling inside and welcomed the invitation. "Did you ever go off in one direction so far that by the time you figured out your mistake, you had no idea how to get back on course?"

"Did you ever wonder why there are sunrises and seasons?" Zac asked. Trevor's face contorted in a way that made it clear he was lost. "Everything around you has a purpose, and most things have more than one. They are there to teach, to guide, to instruct, to gently whisper 'there is more here than what you see.' Spring and sunrise are constant reminders that life follows death, although most people think about it the other way around. Every year there is a fresh start. Every day there is a fresh start. Every hour, minute, or second, there can be a fresh start, and with that start comes new life. What I think people have the most trouble with is that to get to spring, you have to brave winter."

"But what does that even mean in a practical sense?" Trevor questioned.

"It means a lot," Zac said. "You established some pretty firm beliefs early in life because you had to find a way to survive. Some of those beliefs were good, but some have taken you in a bad direction. You never wanted to forgive, largely because you thought you never needed forgiveness. So you kept on, day after day, watching broken relationships fall like dead leaves from a tree as your world grew a little colder. You were always convinced that you were right, that you were judging wisely, and that everyone else was in the wrong. Then one day, today, you realized your folly. You finally understood the choices you were making were not only hurting others, they were hurting you as well, and that being right may not be as important as being in relationship. It is time for winter. That part of you, the piece that you relied on so heavily to get you through some very rough times, it has to die. And if you let it, there will be something wonderful that comes to life in its place. You have to let go of those old, misguided ways if you want to see new life—your Spring. I hate to keep repeating myself, but you do get to choose. This time, however, you have more and better information."

"It's not going to be easy, is it?" Trevor asked. "After all, they call it death for a reason."

Zac smiled. "For some it's not too bad," Zac said. "The others, the ones that don't really want to let go, it can be a very slow and painful process, nothing short of suffering. I guess the big question is, how badly do you want life?"

Trevor said very little during the rest of the meal. He had much to consider. He wondered if he would ever break free from what he had become, or if he even wanted to. There had been times in life he longed to jump out of his skin and become somebody else. Happier. Friendlier. More carefree. More dancing, laughing and singing. Sadly, something in life kept holding him back. Now he wondered what that force was, what was its purpose, and would he ever have the strength to loose its grip?

And then there was Zac, helping and comforting Trevor after being treated so poorly. Giving, almost to a fault, and never asking anything in return.

*Why?*

Trevor was glad this day was almost over. He had woke in Jersey, died once, traveled from a mountaintop to a valley, and had his thinking pulled and twisted like taffy at a carnival. Enough was enough; sleep was more than welcomed.

The room was much nicer than Trevor expected. Sitting on each side of the room was a double bed with matching blankets. There were no night tables, but the sturdy dresser and desk gave the room a homey, old-fashioned feel. But what really made the room inviting, in Trevor's opinion, were the pair of double hung windows near one of the beds. This was just like his bedroom as a child. Trevor used to study the winter stars before he drifted off to sleep, and on rare occasions, watch the early morning sky change slowly from darkness to light. The windows here, however, looked out toward the mountains. It was late now and the night had overcome any trace of color on the ridge, but Trevor could still make out clearly where mountain ended and sky began.

"Would you like to sleep near the window?" Zac asked.

"Yes. Absolutely," Trevor replied. "Thanks. I love watching the stars." He plunked himself down with his feet still on the floor and felt the last of his strength dissipate into the bed.

Zac walked into the bathroom and asked, "How do you feel?"

"Pretty good I guess," he said, just loud enough so Zac could hear him. Trevor's eyes were shut and he could hear the sound of pouring water.

Zac returned carrying a large bowl. "I mean physically, how do you feel?"

Trevor thought for a moment. "Well, my legs are pretty sore, but other than that I'm not too bad."

Zac placed the bowl of water on the floor near Trevor's bed. "Your feet are critical on a hike like this. We need to make sure yours are okay." He began to undo Trevor's laces. Trevor, feeling uncomfortable, could feel his body tighten. After all, the last person to touch his shoe lace was his mother roughly four decades earlier. Zac paid no attention to this body language. He removed Trevor's socks and placed his feet in the bowl of hot water.

"I think you'll sleep well tonight," Zac said.

All Trevor could muster was a groan of agreement. Trevor felt like a child, safe and protected, in sharp contrast to a lifetime spent as a self-made man in a cold and hard world. A tear rolled from his right eye, but he assured himself it had more to do with exhaustion than anything else.

Trevor knew that many of his beliefs were being challenged, and some had already been defeated. He also knew that Zac, a friend walking beside him in this unfamiliar land, was more intentional about relationship than anyone he had known before. Trevor found himself acutely aware of how good this made him feel.

# 5

# The Widows

The two men were on their way long before the sun was visible above the mountains. Trevor would have preferred breakfast at the inn, but Zac insisted he had something better in mind, so they started off along a narrow trail which led to a nearby forest. Trevor stopped, turning for a moment and thinking how strange it was that he would never see the inn again. Then he realized everything on this journey would have two things in common—seen for the first time and seen for the last time. He had never experienced a slice of living that felt so transient, yet there was something in this valley that felt permanent, almost eternal. This land was certainly rich with contradictions, but it was also full of lessons. Trevor wanted to learn.

In less than an hour the two men found themselves at a wooden bridge spanning a large stream. The sun was up now, but still not high enough to be seen through the trees around them. They crossed the bridge and then Zac led them off the trail, following a number of markers he had come to know well over the years. They walked for about fifteen more minutes and saw the forest give way to a large grassy clearing. In the middle of the clearing stood a humble wooden house surrounded by a handful of trees. From a distance it looked to be in some manner of disrepair, with faded yellow paint and moss-stained shingles.

"Are you as hungry as I am?" Zac asked, and immediately started running toward the house.

Trevor, still sore from yesterday, decided the hundred or so yard sprint to the house would do him little harm. He started pumping his arms and legs in an attempt to catch Zac.

When Zac arrived at the house, he stepped up on the weather beaten porch and rang a dinner bell that was mounted near the door. He peeked in through the screen hoping to see movement. Trevor, slightly winded and not too far behind, joined him on the porch.

"Is that you Zac?" called a voice from inside.

"Yes it is," he replied. "Is it too late to get a bite to eat?"

The screen swung open, and out stepped an elderly woman in a well worn dress. Her body had lost the vigor it once held, but her smile lit up the porch more than any sunrise. She grabbed Zac's face in her hands and gave him a strong kiss on the cheek. She held on and looked him in the eye.

"It is so good to see you," she said. "And yes, there is always plenty for a friend. Who is this you brought with you?"

"Nina, I would like you to meet Trevor," Zac said. "I found him up in the mountains yesterday morning."

"Sure you did," Nina said with a wink. "It is very nice to meet you Trevor." She grabbed Trevor's hand and squeezed it hard.

"It's nice to meet you too, ma'am," Trevor said, not really sure what to call the older woman.

"Ma'am? At least someone around here has some manners," Nina teased as she poked Zac in the ribs. She opened the door and the two men followed her inside.

"Where is Annie?" Zac asked.

"I'm in here," Annie called from another room. "Come see me."

"She hasn't been feeling well," Nina said softly.

Zac walked into the bedroom and the other two followed. Annie was sitting up in bed, holding a dog-eared book.

"Zac, did you come to brighten my day?" she asked.

"Yes I did."

"Give me a hug," she demanded, holding her arms out as women secure in their identity so often do. Zac obliged, and then stepped back from the bed to introduce his friend.

"Annie, I want you to meet Trevor."

"I'm honored," she said. "I hope you know you are in good company."

"Yes, I've been getting that impression," Trevor said.

"Nina, why don't you feed these boys some breakfast?" Annie asked.

"I was going to, but you had to interrupt," Nina countered, playfully.

"Can you join us?" Zac asked.

Annie grabbed his hand. "I'd love to, but it's best I stay in bed. It's okay, I have a very nice book to keep me company. But don't leave until you've said goodbye."

"I won't," Zac assured her, and the three moved back into the kitchen.

It was a small room, and everything seemed out of date, but Zac knew that few meals rivaled that which came from these humble beginnings. Trevor was amazed at the energy and efficiency Nina displayed as pots and pans remained in constant motion in what played out to be a cooking decathlon. When it was all over, 20 or 30 minutes later, the small table in the center of the room was filled with a feast. There were pancakes stacked high on one large plate, sausage and bacon on another. Close to a pitcher of orange juice were scrambled eggs, toast, and a number of different flavored jams and jellies, not to mention hot maple syrup–real maple syrup. Each man also had his own oversized cup of fresh brewed coffee.

When Nina finally sat down, she looked across the table and a look of horror filled her face. "Oh dear, I forgot the oatmeal."

Zac grabbed her arm before she could stand up. "This will be fine. Don't you think?" he asked, looking at Trevor.

"More than fine. This is amazing," Trevor said. He reached his fork to grab a pancake, but Nina slapped his hand.

"Do you boys mind if we give thanks before we eat?" Nina spoke her words more like a command than a question.

Zac smiled at her. "Your house, your rules."

"Thank you," she said, and bowed her head to pray. Zac followed her lead but Trevor kept his head up, eyeing the breakfast that would soon be his. "Father, we want to thank you for all our blessings, a house, good food," she raised her head and caught Trevor off guard when she winked at him, "and some really good friends." She dropped her head again and drew a deep breath. "You love us better than we love you. We thank you for that. Please take good care of Annie. Amen." And with that, the feast began. Trevor loaded up a plate full of pancakes while Zac grabbed eggs and toast. Nina

56

seemed more interested with her guests than with the food.

"So tell me about yourself," she said to Trevor.

"Well I work for a telecommunications firm in New Jersey," he said between bites, "but I guess that would be worked. Ever since college I spent my entire career working for the same company, although I did move around the country. I started off in Atlanta, spent four or five years there, and then—"

"Excuse me," Nina interrupted, placing her hand on Trevor's. "I don't really care about what you did to earn a living. I want to hear about you. What are you like? Do you have a family? Good friends? What do you like to do with your time when you aren't working? Do you read? Garden? I want to hear the important stuff."

Trevor grinned. "You'll have to forgive me; old habits die hard."

"That's true," Nina agreed, "but they can die if you let them."

Trevor nodded. "Well, I don't read much, maybe one or two books a year. The only gardening I do is to help my wife at the beginning of the season, after that it's all her. No kids, but I do have a great wife, and I'd have to say in many ways I don't really know what I'm like. Up until yesterday morning I thought I had it figured out, but recently I'm feeling that I may have spent a lifetime being lost."

"Zac can certainly have that effect on a person," she said, and then turned to scold him, jokingly. "Why do you do that to people?" Zac just shrugged his shoulders and continued chewing his toast. "Well you may not know exactly who you are, but I can tell there is something there, something special inside," Nina said. "I can tell things like that. People are always telling me I am a very good judge of character."

The words she spoke left Trevor feeling warm inside. In another world he might have brushed off such a compliment like unwanted flies, but this time he let the praise stick. It felt good, better than good. He looked around the room and wasn't bothered by the peeling paint or the aging furniture. Instead, he focused on the old woman with the inviting smile and the young man so much at home in his own skin. Trevor felt peace, true, unshakable peace, unlike anything he had known before.

Not long afterward, Trevor and Zac found themselves sprawled in Adirondack chairs on the porch. Trevor had eaten too much, and was now paying the price for his lack of discipline.

*What better way to compliment the chef?*

His stomach was bulging, his body lethargic, and a desire to close his eyes was welling up inside. Zac stood up, walked to a nearby shed, and rolled out an old, wooden wheel barrow with a rusty steel wheel. He pushed it near a large woodpile and started loading firewood. Trevor, having thoroughly enjoyed his meal and the comfort of the porch, hardly felt like moving. But how could he just sit and watch Zac repay the favor alone? In no time, Zac was bringing a load to stack against the side of the house.

"Can I help?" Trevor asked, sitting up as if he was ready to work, even though he was much closer to sleep.

"Just relax. I'm only gonna' move one more load," Zac said.

"Okay," Trevor said nonchalantly, but inside he was far more excited about the opportunity to rest. He closed his eyes.

The bell rang and Trevor jumped. He could see Nina standing near the doorway.

"I'm sorry," she said. "I didn't see you there. I thought you were with Zac."

Trevor immediately felt that something was wrong.

*Why would she ring the bell right after breakfast?*

He was still foggy from his nap. He stood up, moved to the edge of the porch, and quickly surveyed the property. There was no sign of Zac. After a few seconds Trevor stepped down off the porch and noticed the sun riding high in the sky, practically overhead. He couldn't believe it. Had he been asleep that long?

"Where is he?" Trevor asked.

"I don't know," Nina said, peering out over the farm. This caused Trevor no small amount of concern as his mind caught hold of a few dark thoughts, that sadly, were never that far out of reach.

*Would Zac really leave without me? Have I been that poor of a sidekick that now he wants to go it alone? Maybe this is payback for last night's betrayal.*

He continued to torment himself until he saw movement far off in the field and the tension in his body slackened. Covered in dirt and sweat, rubbing his hands together to free them of debris, Zac walked toward the house. Trevor hurried out to meet him.

"What's going on?" Trevor asked, "You told me you were only gonna' move two piles of firewood."

"And that's all I moved," Zac insisted, "but then I turned over the garden, gathered up some kindling, milked the cows and goats, fed the chickens—"

"Whoa. Why didn't you wake me?" Trevor protested.

"Annie and Nina are real important to me and I like to help them out whenever I can," Zac said. "I know you would have helped, but I'm glad you took a nap. You needed the rest."

"It's not right," Trevor said.

"Why?" Zac asked. "Because you didn't work as hard as I did? Because you lost some silly competition in your head? I did this to help a friend, not because I'm driven by some unquenchable force that has no concern for my well being. You don't need to live that way anymore. You have nothing to prove here, or anywhere else. I don't expect anything from you. I only want the best for you, and I can guarantee that our friends inside that house want the same."

Trevor's face revealed the struggle inside. He turned and walked a few steps away. Why was he so unable, or unwilling, to think healthy thoughts? Why did battles from wars started elsewhere need to follow him here? Why couldn't it be easier? He turned to Zac.

"I'm not very good at this, am I?" Trevor asked.

Zac closed the gap between them and placed his hands on Trevor's shoulders. "I wish you could see yourself the way I see you, not full of faults and failures, but promise and possibilities. There is a great man inside of you that longs to break out. Why do you keep listening to lies? Lies that condemn. Lies that beat down. Do you have any idea what it means to be loved unconditionally? Any idea how freeing that can be?"

"Of course I do." Trevor didn't feel good about lying, but he

60

didn't know what else to do.

"No," Zac protested, "You really don't. But love is much stronger than the lies you believe. I hope you will understand before our time is over."

Zac placed his hand on the back of Trevor's neck and gently nudged him along toward the house. Once inside, they found large bowls of chicken soup and home baked bread waiting for them on the table. Zac said a quick prayer and then everyone dug in.

"It looks like you got a lot done out there," Nina said.

"I think so," Zac said. "Next time out I need to work on that chicken coop."

"You take good care of us," Nina said. "Thank you." She looked over at Trevor. He was quiet and glum. "Trevor, I'm glad you had a chance to rest. You must have had a tough day yesterday."

"I shouldn't have been that tired," Trevor said. "I should have helped."

Nina filled the room with her smile. "No, I don't think you should have," she said. "I think it was best for you to take it easy. I know you're a hard worker, I can tell, but I think it was good for you to slow down. You need to learn how important it is to rest. It really is okay."

Trevor wasn't sure what to say or think. He tried to spend the remainder of lunchtime in self-condemnation, but it was difficult. Zac and Nina proved a formidable source of encouragement and their words were sincere. It made Trevor think about his high school physics class, where he learned that the smallest trace of light can penetrate darkness, but no amount of darkness can hinder light; a strange dichotomy.

"That was great," Zac said at the conclusion of the meal. "Let me help clean up."

"You will do no such thing," Nina scolded. "You did all that hard work outside and now you need to be on your way. You still have a long way to go."

Zac grinned at her. There was something real in this relationship, something significant. Trevor wasn't clear on how to build relationships like this, but he desperately wanted to experience them.

When Zac excused himself to say goodbye to Annie, Trevor felt somewhat awkward being alone with Nina. She recognized the discomfort and busied herself packing up a few treats for the men to take with them on their journey.

"Do you like raisins?" she asked with her back turned toward him.

"Yes I do," he said. She wrapped a cupful in a small napkin and placed it into a larger bag.

"Peanuts?" she asked.

"Sure," he replied. Nina repeated the process.

"And how about my award-winning homemade pretzels?"

"I can't imagine why I wouldn't," Trevor said. She dropped half a dozen into the bag and then turned to him with a smile on her face.

"Here," she said, handing him the bag and wrapping her hands around his. "This is me doing a favor for you. Now I want you to do a favor for me. Can you do that for me, Trevor?"

"Certainly," he said, never imagining she might step beyond propriety to make her request.

She reached up and held his face between her hands the way a loving grandmother might. "Can you stop fighting?" she asked. "There is a tidal wave of love poised to overwhelm you. It wants to sweep you up and carry you to new and better places, to release you, but it won't happen unless you let it. Can you let go of the image, and the rules, and the scars, and whatever else is holding you back from honestly experiencing all that life has to offer? Can you just let go?"

Zac returned before Trevor could respond. Trevor wasn't sure if her questions demanded answers, or if they were just Nina's way of making a very direct point. He handed the bag of food to Zac and then wrapped his arms around Nina giving her a long and thoughtful hug. This had never been Trevor's style, but it was the best gift he could give to her at that moment and so he gave it freely.

Nina kissed both men goodbye, held open the creaky screen door, and they were on their way. As they walked from the house, both men heard the familiar sound of clanging dishes and started laughing.

# 6

# A Very Good Day

They hiked well into the afternoon before the forest finally gave way to clearing–an endless field of tall grass, as green an image as anything Trevor could remember. The men stopped for a moment and watched the grass as it was kissed by the wind. Currents of air rolling gently, one after the other, across the meadow, looked like waves upon the sea. Trevor was very much a stranger to this land, yet could not help but marvel at its beauty. Images from childhood flashed into his brain, and yes, he could remember the innocence, the serenity, the inspiration. So much was still quite fresh in his mind, and now he was a child again. The cares of the world were behind him, nothing but peace ahead. He was home.

Trevor started off again, holding out his arms like wings, skimming them across the surface of this sea of grass. He found himself fascinated by the tiny dance made by each stalk as his hand brushed by, and failed to notice the smile on Zac's face. Decades of cynicism and disregard were now replaced with wonder and appreciation. He had no no work to accomplish, no bills to pay, no appointments to keep, and no one to answer to. He was free, more so than he knew was possible.

The sun beat down upon his body, and having recently survived a harsh New Jersey winter, Trevor welcomed the chance to feel its warmth again. In no time at all, the sweat was rolling down his neck and soaking into his shirt; a much better alternative to hats and gloves. He and Zac stopped a couple of times, shedding layers of clothing, until they found themselves in t-shirts.

Most of Trevor's aches from a day ago were forgotten now, and the two men maintained a relaxed pace. At some point, without a word, Trevor dropped his backpack and submerged into the tall grass, laying his body on the ground. There, looking up through the opening carved by his body, he caught sight of a rich blue sky. Zac followed Trevor's lead and hit the ground just a few feet away.

Minutes passed in silence.

"Sometimes I forget how beautiful it is," Trevor said.

"Distraction," Zac said.

"Understatement," Trevor confirmed. They listened to the wind rushing over a million stalks of grass and for the first time Trevor noticed how musical it sounded. He watched carefully as each small blade played part in a much larger score. He closed his eyes and let the music bathe him.

Eventually Zac spoke up. "I like trying to figure out what the clouds are, like that one over there. That's got to be a seagull."

"I forgot about that," Trevor said. "When I was a kid, a friend and I used to go to a merry-go-round near my house. We'd lie on our backs for hours and play this game, at least it seemed like hours. I don't see the wings."

"That's because he's on the ground," Zac said. "You can see his legs and tail feathers."

"I see it," Trevor said with excitement. He could feel his body,

65

like the universe, expanding. No longer held together tightly by destructive forces, he was now radiating outward to take on an entirely new form. "Were we meant to live like this in the old world?"

Zac laughed lightly. "That old world you speak of is only a day away, but I think your question has merit. Hard work and responsibility are great things, but if you lose the ability to be young then a big piece of life has been lost."

"Yeah," Trevor said, exhaling as if for the last time. He watched a few more clouds roll by and thought one looked like an oddly shaped car. He said nothing, having more important matters to discuss. "Where are we going?"

"To the mountains," Zac said.

"I get that part of it, but everything with you has a purpose," Trevor said. "This seems like more than just a hike. This is a journey, isn't it?"

"Always thinking," Zac said. He sat up and peered through the grass toward Trevor. "I'm glad you're listening. I can tell you're learning. I hope you keep on questioning. As for the journey, that's really up to you."

Trevor, still on his back, smiled up at the sky. He had met a man who spoke words like a flame. On the surface, even after short exposure, they made an impact, being full of wisdom and clarity. But inside at the core, after deeper reflection, the heat was far more intense and most life changing. Trevor closed his eyes. He thought about the man he had always been, as well as the man he might enjoy becoming. He considered paupers, captains and kings, and how alike they really were. And then he held his breath, just to prove to himself that he still could.

"I have an idea," Zac said, unable to check his exhilaration. In a flash he was on his feet and running. Trevor jumped up and saw the younger man bounding through the high grass. Trevor did the best he could to catch up, but hindered by a trace of fatigue and the bounce of his backpack, he fell further behind.

Zac stopped after a long sprint. Trevor slowed to a walk, struggling for breath. He noticed a large pond behind Zac. By the time Trevor reached the water, Zac was standing in his boxer shorts on the dry end of a small dock.

"Are you kidding me?" Trevor asked.

Zac started running like an eight year old at camp and catapulted himself off the dock. As he surfaced, he let out a yelp for the entire valley to hear.

Trevor already had his shoes off and seconds later was running down the dock with a scream of his own. In he plunged, but resurfaced milliseconds later. Every square inch of his skin felt like it was burning or freezing in the frigid water; he couldn't tell for sure. Even worse, his brain hurt. He swam as fast as he could for the dock and looked more flying fish than human as he made his exit. His breath was quick and strong. After an intense 17 second workout, Trevor lay face down on the weathered boards like a seal lazing in the sunshine. He wondered how it was possible that there was no visible ice on the surface of the pond.

Zac swam to the dock and lifted himself out of the water. He stood near Trevor, careful not to block the sun, looking down and laughing. "I've never seen you move so fast."

"Freezer brain," Trevor mumbled with his face buried in the dock. "Pain." He was pressing his hands vice-like against each side of his skull as he rolled onto his back. The two men shared the laughter of lifelong friends. Zac sat down on the dock, dangling his feet off the edge and into the water. He moved them back and forth, attracting the attention of one or two aggressive fish.

"You were right," Zac said.

"I know. It's freezing."

"Yes, but that's not what I'm talking about. This is a journey, but it's up to you to make the most of it. Up to you to discover the mistakes of a lifetime, to find new ways to think, to relate, to move in a better direction."

"And what if I screw it up again?" Trevor asked.

"I guess you have two options," Zac said. "You can live in fear, afraid of yesterday's mistakes, thinking that somehow yesterday can dictate tomorrow. But if you do, remember that fear is a monster with many faces, seeking to destroy. The other option is to live with hope, trusting that no matter how things look or feel at any given moment, they will work out fine in the end; and as much as it flies in the face of logic, learn to put hope before reason."

Trevor sat up and for the first time in forever didn't care that his stomach stuck out well beyond his shorts. "You make it sound easy but I'm not so sure I would even recognize fear. I can look back now and see some of it, how it drove me one way or the other, but at the time I considered myself fearless."

Zac nodded in agreement. "Maybe you were, but you are already a very different man, and these are very different days. Let me ask you this, if you could have anything right now, what would it be?"

"That's weird," Trevor said. "I've actually been thinking along those lines, asking myself what is missing? I really have two answers. First, I want to be a better man. You've inspired me to want that of myself. There's something there, and I can't put my finger on it just yet, but it's motivating me, pushing me to a better place. Second, and maybe it's tied to the first thing, I want some really good friends. I'm not just talking about the guys that you go out to lunch with at work, or have a few beers with during a big game. I'm talking about the people that are there when your basement floods. The ones that stop over unannounced after dinner with dessert. The people you would be happy to go on vacation with, not because you have to, but because it makes it a great trip. I guess I just want to taste some of the things I missed my first time through."

"That's a pretty good answer. Now comes the harder question. What keeps you from getting what you want?" Zac asked.

"Not really sure. I'm thinking it must be hard to improve like that, to continually think and act in the best interest of others. It seems a lot easier to be selfish, make fun of people, and get angry. As for relationships, I just don't think everyone was cut from the same fabric. I think it must be easier for some people to have great relationships. Not so sure it's that way for me."

At that moment, Trevor noticed a number of gruesome scars running across Zac's back. Each cut deep into his skin, and in some areas it was clear that muscle had been torn as well. Whatever produced these wounds had obviously done its work a long time ago because the discoloration looked faded now.

"What happened?" Trevor asked.

Zac turned and followed Trevor's eyes with his own. "It's a long story," Zac said, somewhat disinterested. "Maybe another time. But let me get this straight, you think everyone else has the relationship thing figured out and you're the only one struggling?"

"I didn't say the only one," Trevor said. "Just one of a select few." Both men laughed.

"Seems that most of the people I come across are ruled by fear when it comes to relationships," Zac said. "Fear of rejection, fear of intimacy, fear of giving everything they have. It's just fear. Try to remember the last time you were relaxed enough to present a completely unaltered version of yourself to someone else. When you weren't checking your words, analyzing reactions, or hiding behind a well crafted disguise. All those calculations that go on in your head can keep you from true relationship. Everyone does it to some extent, but every once in a while you find someone who uses a completely different type of math. Someone who shares a kind word, knowing it may brighten someone else's day. Someone who admits failure or grants forgiveness, because it may help bring pardon to a guilty soul. Someone who offers friendship, love, and intimacy, knowing full well that offer could be met with rejection. It does take courage, but if you can stare down the fear you will probably find most of what you are looking for."

"I guess it makes sense," Trevor said. "But what about being a better man?"

"Better relationships will get you well on your way to being a better man," Zac said.

Trevor leaned his body back down against the dock, wandering deep in thought as the sun shone down upon his chest and warmed his soul.

They pushed on that afternoon over rich grasslands and farms, through forests filled with birch and maple, across a river or stream (each man held a different opinion), into more fields, and eventually climbed atop a small knoll where they set up their bed rolls. Trevor could see mountains to the east and mountains to the west, a beginning and an end. He had only been here a couple of days but was already understanding how much he would miss this place–how much he would miss his friend.

Trevor thought about his wife and recognized how different things had become. He missed her. He also realized how much he cared for her. He wondered how she was doing. It had been only two days and he understood she must be going through a rough time now. Would she be okay? Did she miss him? It would be a different life now, but Trevor desperately wanted the best for her: good friends, enlightening conversation, warm spring evenings with beautiful sunsets. All the best that life, that other life, had to offer.

Trevor considered some of the people in his path a single lifetime ago, those he called his friends and those he called his enemies. Would anyone remember him? Would anyone smile when they heard his name? Would anyone feel like a better man or woman for having known him? It was terribly ironic that death became the place where Trevor finally started learning how to live.

And so he stood, statue-like on the knoll, staring off toward the setting sun as it touched the mountains. They were not that far away.

"So how do you like it here?" Zac asked.

Trevor refocused. "It's incredible."

"A few days ago you may not have been able to imagine this place," Zac said. "More importantly, what can you imagine now?"

The two men locked stares while Trevor tried to absorb the breadth and depth of Zac's words. Trevor looked back toward the mountains and watched the sun disappear.

# 7

# Smithfield

It was a slow morning. Neither man woke before sunrise and breakfast was anything but rushed. When the sun finally appeared over the mountains, Zac stood up. "I guess it's time we got started," he said. Trevor agreed, and not long afterward they were on their way.

From what Trevor remembered of his running days, he expected today to be his worst, but whether it was the tempered pace or the clean air, he felt pretty good. His calves and thighs were still a little tight, but they felt strong and capable.

It was late afternoon when the pair decided to call it quits. There was still plenty of daylight left but Smithfield made an ideal stopping point. They had pushed through a fair number of miles, so a hearty meal and good night's rest would serve them well.

Smithfield was misplaced in time, the blacksmith's shop gave that away immediately, as the music of steel on steel filled the air when they entered town. Not far down the wide dirt road they passed a large mercantile which served up most of what the people needed, and a saloon which served up some of what they didn't. There was a row of buildings lining each side of the street. Most were painted, but some stood gray and bare against the elements. The handful of people that were out and about waved hello to the travelers.

Trevor followed Zac toward *The Bread Basket*, a small

restaurant with authentic home cooking and a few rooms for rent on the second floor. Before they could make it to the front porch, two large men, hardened by time and pressure, approached them. The only thing striking about them was that each appeared a little tougher than the other.

"You guys lookin' for some work?" one asked. Although he was physically intimidating, his voice had a calming quality that immediately put Trevor at ease.

"Not me," Zac said, " I have plenty to keep me busy."

"What about you?" the other asked, looking directly at Trevor. "I'm Jacob, by the way. This is my brother Jeremy."

"I don't think I can," Trevor said, imagining that everyone knew he was only passing through.

"Why not?" Jacob asked.

"I, uh," Trevor stammered, not quite sure if he knew the answer. He looked over at Zac hoping he would chime in, but eventually finished his thought. "I think I need to stay with him."

"That sounds pretty weird," Jacob said. "We've got some good farm work. Make a man out of you. The pay is fair, and you'll get plenty of food and a place to stay. How 'bout it?"

Trevor looked at Zac, not sure what to think.

"I would never tell you what you had to do," Zac replied. "You've always had the right to choose."

This surprised Trevor. Up until this point he could not have imagined being anywhere other than with Zac, but freedom is a very strong word. His mind danced. What adventures could he find in this land of rugged beauty? What discoveries might he make if given the chance to explore, and not just follow? How might the hours roll into days and weeks if he were to set off on his own in any direction he chose?

"I think I'll have to pass," Trevor said, hardly convincing anyone with his answer, certainly not himself.

"We're just over that way, not far from town, in case you change your mind," Jacob said, pointing beyond a small white school house. And with that they walked away.

Zac made his way up onto the front porch and in through the door. Trevor lingered, watching the men for a few seconds and then caught up with Zac. They were greeted by a woman behind the desk. She looked to be well into her 40s, but the orange fire had not faded from her hair.

"Hello stranger," she said. "Where have you been?"

"Somewhere between point A and point B," Zac said. The two giggled. "But you've got to know I'll always find my way back for more of those mashed potatoes."

"Yes I do," she said. "And for tonight, a room with two beds?"

"That sounds great," Zac said. "Missy, I'd like you to meet a friend of mine. This is Trevor."

She reached out her hand with sincere hospitality and Trevor grabbed hers in return. "Pleasure to meet you Trevor," she said. "How do you like our valley?"

"I love it," Trevor said. "Easy to see why anyone would want to call it home."

"Just like bugs on a pie," she said while jotting down a few words in a large guest book. "It is a very good place to be, but maybe you already know that." She turned to Zac. "That'll be six dollars please."

Zac dug into his pack and pulled out a small bag filled with twenty silver dollars. He proceeded to drop six of them into Missy's hand. He closed the bag tightly and gave it a small shake, knowing he had plenty left for dinner and a few additional supplies to help them on their way.

"Dinner at the usual hour?" Zac asked.

"Anytime after five," she said, "and let me know if there is anything I can do to make you fellas feel more at home."

The two men sat quietly, enjoying their meal. Both men had fried chicken, a large pile of mashed potatoes, and green beans on their plate. There were only a few people in the dining room, and Trevor found himself fascinated by the atmosphere. There were sturdy wooden tables and chairs, tablecloths and napkins made from real cloth, silverware that really was, and plates so thick they could break a toe if one fell on a foot. Everything seemed more real and substantive than what Trevor was used to. Different in a good way, much like Zac.

They were not even halfway through dinner when Trevor was shaken from his thoughts by a commotion outside. Zac dropped his fork and ran to the window.

"Charlie," he said with dismay, and then made a run for the door. Trevor, uncertain he would get back to his meal again, quickly swallowed a fork full and gave chase.

Zac was waiting at the entry to a wide alley between *The Bread Basket* and a dress shop when Trevor caught up. He could see a young boy surrounded by three larger boys. They had blocked off any hope of escape and were not shy about their taunting. Zac stood unnoticed.

"Why don't you go back where you came from?" Charlie shouted. He was obviously the leader of the mob, and the other two knew their place in the pecking order. The young boy said nothing, enraging Charlie even more.

"I said get out of here," Charlie demanded, knowing quite well there was no way for the younger boy to leave. Charlie shoved him into the side of the building. His shoulder blades hit hard and then his head snapped back, catching the edge of a clapboard. It jarred a tear from his eye and onto his cheek.

"You talk funny, you look funny, and no one wants you here," Charlie continued and then leaned in, putting his face uncomfortably close to the young boy's. "Get it?" he said, hoping to intimidate more than he already had.

Trevor took a step in their direction to intervene, but Zac held him back and stepped into the skirmish by himself. The boys immediately froze. Zac was easily recognized in these parts, but not much was known about him, at least in certain circles. No one was quite sure what to expect. Charlie backed away one or two steps. Zac entered the space between the boys, gently squeezing the shoulder of one of the gang on the way in. Kneeling down near Charlie and the younger boy, Zac brushed his hand over the ground. No one said a word. Slowly, methodically, Zac wrote letters in the dirt. T-O-R-N.

He looked up, studying the face of each antagonist. Not one of them understood what was happening. He continued. P-A-G-E. Zac kept his eyes on the ground now. The words remained there for almost half a minute, and then another brush of his hand and they were gone. Zac rose to his feet.

Charlie bit his lip. He tried desperately to keep his emotions in check and then rubbed something from his eye. "I got dinner waitin'," he said, and tore off away from the conflict. The other two boys looked at one another. One shrugged his shoulders and then they both walked away as well, looking somewhat unsure over what was happening.

The young boy stood there with his back against the building. He was somewhat relieved, but still unsure and afraid.

"It's okay now" Zac said, placing his hand on the young boy's shoulder. "What's your name?"

"Michael," he said timidly.

"Where is your mother?"

Zac, Trevor, and the young boy entered the sheriff's office and immediately looked to the jail cell. Michael quickly ran to his mother, hugging as much of her as he could reach through the bars. Her eyes welled up with tears, but she tried to be strong.

"Good evening sheriff," Zac said.

"Look who's back in town," the sheriff said with a touch of disdain. "What can I do for you?"

"Well, my friend and I stumbled across young Michael here out in the street," Zac said. "I was just a little curious why his mom was locked up."

"Theft," the sheriff said in a loud voice. "She was doing some cleaning for a well to do gentleman in town and tried to run off with some of his stuff. We don't take that kind of thing too lightly around here."

"I can appreciate that," Zac said, "but can you tell me specifically what she stole?"

"What difference does it make?" the sheriff said with venom, "Stealin' is stealin'."

"Yes, I understand," Zac said, "but sometimes we lose sight of the gray in a world that clings tightly to black-and-white. Wouldn't you agree?"

The sheriff stared hard at Zac. Both men knew the rumors. Both men knew the truth. More importantly, both men avoided speaking about the sheriff's recent struggle with alcohol and the difficult road which brought him there.

"What's that suppose to mean?" the sheriff asked, somewhat fired up by what he considered insinuation. He had been an upstanding citizen, not that long ago, but when his wife ran off with another man, the sheriff's life spun out of control. Since that day he began a slow and steady march toward bitterness and alienation. It recently became more his pleasure than his duty to punish others over the slightest of infractions, and was often overheard mumbling something about the letter of the law.

"What I mean," Zac began, "is that sometimes when you look between the two places we call right and wrong, you often find a lot more right and a lot less wrong. I know a fair number of people

79

who have had an unflattering label placed on them because they did something they shouldn't have, even though it's exactly what most of us would do in that very same situation."

"Guess your gonna' make me look for that report," the sheriff said grudgingly, reaching across his desk to pick up a small pile of papers.

"It's probably time we got past the hearsay and false accusations, and tried to set things straight for everybody's sake. Don't you think?"

The sheriff's demeanor changed in an instant when he realized that help was here for him. He wasn't alone anymore. His longtime friend had returned. The two men shared a smile, something the sheriff's face hadn't seen in months.

"I know I haven't been around for a while," Zac said, "but I also know we can get through this together." Zac reached out his hand and grabbed the sheriff's wrist as a sign of strength and support.

Trevor stood like a spectator. This man with no last name, most likely without a proper home, had become more than just a fascination; he was an enigma. Trevor found it inspiring that such a simple man, with no discernible ambition or agenda, could be so profound and impacting. It was undeniable that wherever Zac stepped, someone's life seemed to change, and always for the better.

The sheriff beat his fist against the front door of the largest house in town. It took longer than anyone expected, but eventually the door swung open and John Fitzgerald stood there with a large cigar in his hand.

"Yeah?" was all he could be troubled to say.

"Sorry to bother you John," the sheriff said, "but I found this woman in the cell when I got back from my afternoon rounds. I didn't get a chance to talk to my deputy before he left for the day and I was just wonderin' if you had some time to talk this out?"

"Not right now," John replied and attempted to close the door.

"I think you'd better make some time," the sheriff demanded, placing his foot in the doorway. John reluctantly stepped out onto the porch. "Why don't you tell me what happened today?"

"Gladly," John replied with burning sarcasm. "I had hired this young lady to come and clean my house based on the recommendation of a friend. I'm not usually one to entertain the employment of vagrants, but I thought, *how bad could she be?* Besides, we had to let our previous maid go and the house really needed a cleaning. So, I gave her a chance. She spent a few hours tooling around the place, trying to look busy. When I eventually figured out what was going on, or more importantly, what wasn't, I paid her for her time and she left. I went upstairs for a few minutes, and when I came back down I found her in the kitchen stealing a loaf of bread. Can you imagine? You just can't trust these people."

"And that's the absolute truth?" Zac asked defiantly.

"Are you calling me a liar?" John asked, pointing his cigar in Zac's direction.

"I'm not calling you anything, but I am asking. Are you lying?" There was an uncomfortable silence. "I heard a much

81

different version of this story," Zac said.

"Do tell," John said, "I am riveted."

"The other version tells of a poor woman going to work in the home of a wealthy businessman. The woman has nothing, and desperately needs her wages at the end of each day to feed and provide shelter for herself and her young boy. After six hours of hard work, the woman is told she will get no pay. Having broken some worthless trinket, she must pay a penalty to the richest man in town. Does that story sound familiar?"

"You're insane," John said. Silence overtook both men. The air between them grew charged, each refusing to take his eyes off the other.

Sensing an impasse, the sheriff stepped in. "Look John, is there anything we can do here? She really needs to take care of her boy."

"I'm a reasonable man and always willing to make a compromise," John said. "Ten dollars and I'll drop the charges."

"It was a lousy loaf of bread," Trevor called out, unable to contain his frustration over such a deceitful miser any longer. This was probably the first person he had met in the valley whom he genuinely disliked. He wondered if it was time to bring hate back into his vocabulary. "All you want to do is take advantage of this situation, of every situation."

"And how do you know that?" John asked.

Trevor paused. He looked around at the others on the porch, somewhat ashamed of who he was. "Because I was just like you," he confessed. "I didn't care if people lost their jobs, their friends, or even their happiness. None of that mattered to me, but it should have," he finished, seemingly deflated. He stepped off the porch to be alone and watched from the corner of his eye.

"I'll pay it," Zac said. John smirked, caring less about the money and more about coming out on top again. Trevor fumed. None of it seemed right. This play was all too familiar; the rich dominating the poor, the powerful controlling the weak. He wanted there to be justice, if not in his world, at least in the next. He was surprised that Zac would back down so easily, that there was so little fight in him. Zac pulled the bag of coins from his pocket and counted away most of what was left.

It was what it was, and in the final accounting John Fitzgerald was paid 10 silver dollars to have his house cleaned by a meticulous servant. Michael and his mom were together again with four dollars and a loaf of bread. As for Zac and Trevor, their money had dried up and there was nothing left to cover the cost of their meal. Fortunately Zac had a few trade skills he seldom spoke about.

The last few moments of daylight were fading. Trevor had one end of a clapboard pressed against the building while Zac held the other. A small oil lamp sat on a step ladder behind them providing just enough light to finish their work.

"What do you think?" Zac asked. Trevor leaned back a bit so his eyes could follow the line of the board in relation to the one below it.

"Looks level to me," Trevor said, and with that, Zac began driving nails into the board. Trevor reached to the ground for the

83

final piece of siding. "I never met anyone like you. You're like a runaway train of love and compassion. How did you get like that?"

"I guess it's just part of my nature," Zac said, keeping his eyes on his work.

"It just seems so different from what I'm used to. I think I'd like to be more that way," Trevor confessed. "I've always been so self-consumed."

Zac stopped his hammering, stood straight and stared deeply at Trevor. Trevor felt exposed and uncertain.

"Not many ever get to the place of voicing words like that, of looking beyond themselves, seeing the pain of those around them, and wondering if there is anything they can do to help someone else carry a burden. I have never been more impressed with you than I am right now."

Trevor was stunned. Uncertainty left him, replaced by the joy of a young boy held high in the air by an approving father. His vision blurred as tears formed in his eyes. A few broke free and rolled down his face.

Zac dropped the hammer, walked to Trevor and wrapped his arms around him. The two men stood together in the light of the oil lamp. It was as if two brothers separated during a horrific battle, tired, wounded and introspective, were reunited the next day to celebrate victory. This was how relationship was meant to be, and in that spectacular moment, Trevor felt more like a child and more like a man than ever before. He felt a connection to, and an understanding of, a universe that had so often been hidden.

When the two men separated Trevor wiped his cheeks dry,

not because he felt the need to keep up appearances, but merely to remove the moisture that tickled his skin.

"Why did you write *torn page* in the dirt back there?" Trevor asked.

Zac, appearing somewhat distracted, walked to the building and began inspecting the newly added siding. "Charlie isn't a bad kid. He's just living through a real tough time right now. His dad is pretty hard on him. The end of each day is usually met with a few lashes from the belt for some wrong only a ravenous father could find. His mom tries to give him a spark from time to time, but a father can make an unmistakable impact on a young boy's life."

Trevor swallowed hard. He could feel the sting of reality deep in his core. The memories were still fresh enough to cause pain.

"But it's not just at night that Charlie gets beat down," Zac said. "His dad likes to torment him during the day whenever he gets the chance. One of his favorite nicknames, maggot, he uses to remind his son that he is small, insignificant, and constantly feeding off someone else. Not long ago he tore a page from a book and nailed it to Charlie's wall. It was a drawing of a maggot. Pretty nice, huh? I didn't want Charlie to feel bad, but I did want him to recognize how Michael was feeling. I think he understood."

"I'm sure he did," Trevor said. He set the last clapboard into place. Zac picked up the hammer and began nailing again. "My dad was kind of like that," Trevor admitted, "doing most of what he could to try and keep me down."

"I'd like to hear about it sometime. It must have been tough on you," Zac said, driving the last few nails into the siding.

# 8

## Sleepless

Trevor woke, gradually becoming aware of the darkness that surrounded him. His thoughts were fuzzy. This was a routine that Trevor became used to in the old world, so his mind naturally drifted back to his bedroom in New Jersey. He struggled for several moments between fact and fiction, reality and imagination, one world and the next. Lazily reaching out his right arm, he was hoping to touch the curve of his wife's hip. She wasn't there. As his arm fell off the side of the bed he knew something was not right. He quickly realized what the problem was.

Trevor lay there for a few minutes, aware of the extreme silence around him. It was quiet, too quiet. Something was wrong. He strained to hear the sound that never came.

Trevor was wide awake now. It was obvious that Zac had passed all the initial tests of integrity, credibility, and even honor, but in many ways he was still a mystery—far too unknown to instill comfort. Trevor had been drawn to Zac based on many of the virtues of a wise and kindly grandfather, but some of his less predictable characteristics brought concern, and even a tinge of fear. Trevor's mind shuffled through a handful of conspiracy theories as he walked down the hallway, wondering where Zac had gone. By the time he reached the top of the stairway he knew exactly what he had to do.

Stepping onto the front porch, Trevor was willing to concede that exploring an unknown street in bare feet at 2 A.M. might not be the best idea. Wolves, bears, or even a skunk could all prove disastrous. He also had no clue what kind of people might be roaming about. Far greater than his fear, however, was the strength of his curiosity.

*Where is he?*

As he moved slowly onto the dirt road he could only detect two sounds. First, the almost inaudible sound of feet pressing into the clay like surface below him. Second, the deafening beat of the heart inside his chest. He looked to his right, staring down a street he could not see, hoping his eyes might find a way to penetrate absolute darkness. He convinced himself he could identify buildings along the street, but was drawing them more from memory than sight. Looking in the other direction he detected more of the same, but his vision was improving. He stared harder into the night, certain now he could see movement down the road. His eyes locked onto a target.

*Is that the figure of a man or a beast?*

There was most definitely a face, but what it belonged to he could not say. Trevor stood motionless, wondering why he wasn't upstairs in bed. The shadow moved slowly and steadily toward him. Time stalled as the image stopped, perhaps 10 yards away.

"What are you doing out of bed?" Zac asked in a soft voice, designed not to wake anyone. Trevor let out a sigh. Both men moved closer.

"I didn't know where you were," Trevor said. "What are you

doing?"

"I come out here sometimes in the empty hours of the morning to experience stillness. There's no other time of the day that gives you this. It's quiet enough so a person can think without distractions, and sometimes if you really detach, you can hear the things you need to hear most."

"What do you mean?" Trevor asked.

"Come on," Zac said, "Let's walk." He headed back in the direction from where he came.

"Shouldn't we be getting some rest?" Trevor asked, feet still planted on the ground.

Zac stopped. "Shouldn't we be living our lives without worrying about a schedule? There are many steps to take in a lifetime, but there are also moments to capture, experience and enjoy. Let's grab ourselves a moment."

Trevor relented, but the ticking in his head would not die. It would have been a good time to follow Zac's lead, to be quiet and still, but his brain continued processing thought like a quantum computer. This was a hard time of the night for Trevor. It had been for years. He wanted his mind to stop, or at the very least decelerate, but it refused.

*Why am I so compelled to live under such a burden?*

They walked through the side of town that Trevor had not seen before. He could make out a few more stores, a small bank and a stable. Their steps were slow and the silence of the night was pervasive, still Trevor's mind kept churning.

"You don't breathe like a man at peace," Zac said.

"I guess I've got a few thoughts bouncing around upstairs," Trevor said. And he did. Since his reality had been turned upside down only a few short days ago, Trevor had been trying to improve, trying hard to be the better man he talked about. But change did not come as quickly or as easily as expected. Trevor still felt anger, the episode with the honorable Mr. Fitzgerald assured him of that. He still held strong opinions about himself and others, and was convinced he could have managed the sheriff's downturn with greater discipline. Trevor had finally reached a point where he could acknowledge and accept ownership of his shortcomings, but now his inability to change stood as an even greater failure. The ruts established early in life now seemed much harder to break free from than he imagined.

Having lived more than 40 years in a world that demanded and rewarded confidence, Trevor always felt that his was in adequate supply, but questioned that now. He was no longer certain of his ability to overcome hurdles, mishaps, and bad intentions to become the man that he wanted to be. He had already identified a handful of diseased traits worth purging from his life, but he lacked the energy or ambition to eradicate them. Although to most, a session of mental gymnastics such as this might have seemed like useless toil, it served as a crushing blow for a self made man bent on controlling his own destiny. In stark contrast to Zac, Trevor found a way to use the serenity of the night to wage war against himself on the battlefield of his mind.

"It seems like every time I come through here there is a new building," Zac said. "I wonder how long it took to build this town."

"At least a couple of years," Trevor said, still lost in his own cerebral conflict.

"Really?" Zac asked. "You don't think they built it all at once?"

"No," Trevor said, slightly more engaged. He was wondering why Zac would ask something so ridiculous. "It probably started with the store, so farmers in the area could get supplies. Then over time, as more people started doing business, other shops could open. There had to be a blacksmith, so horses could have shoes. Then maybe a saloon, where people could let loose. A bank. A dress shop. Little by little, it all came together. It couldn't just happen all at once."

Zac kept silent for a few seconds. The two men walked step for step until Zac stopped in his tracks. Two steps later Trevor stopped too, not exactly sure why. He turned and looked in Zac's direction, still unable to distinguish facial features in the night.

"It couldn't just happen all at once?" Zac asked.

Trevor stared more intently at Zac, hoping to observe as much of his thinking as he felt Zac had seen of his. He wondered, not for the first time, if this man from the mountains could actually read his mind. It was unnerving. This village took months and years to establish, so what made Trevor think that decades of bad habits forged atop lies and misinformation could be wiped away in an instant with something better left in its place? Why would he enter into this new life, a life full of freedom and possibilities, only to bow down before a new taskmaster that demanded immediate transformation? Perhaps in this world Trevor needed to allow himself to be human, accepting today's flaws while moving toward something better.

"I just want to get it right this time," Trevor said.

"I know you do," Zac said. "Unfortunately, there's often not much separating ambition from compulsion, and few realize where one leaves off and the other begins."

Trevor started walking again, feeling confused and disoriented. Even in darkness his feet seemed capable of walking a straight path, but the trail of thought in his head kept on bending.

"Is there any way to break free of all this?" Trevor asked. "I would love to be comfortable in my own skin and stop worrying about stuff that doesn't even matter."

"I've heard a lot of people talk about freedom over the years," Zac said, "but few understand what it really means. Some try to define it, start taking steps to experience it, but before long most have just found their way into a different set of shackles. The weird thing about freedom is that it's so simple. Most of us have a tendency to over complicate, over analyze. There isn't one thing you've seen me do in the last couple of days that you couldn't have pulled off in preschool."

They moved near the edge of town and Trevor noticed a pile of tree trunks just outside the saw mill. He thought for a moment about what it would be like to live in a place like this, working a mill, a farm, or maybe even in a shop. Could life really be slower? Simpler? Could Mayberry actually exist? He wondered what it must be like to work a job at a pace he could sustain, a pace that would allow for smiles, laughter and even friends. He looked up at the sky, disappointed the stars were now tucked behind cloud cover, and felt a sudden burst of sadness.

"Maybe I'm not cut out for this," Trevor said. "Maybe other people have a better understanding of how to slow down, how to relax, how to stop living under the gun."

"Why are you so hard on yourself?" Zac asked. "Over the past couple of days you've recognized some of the mistakes you've made in the past, and you've tried to make a few adjustments. It's not always easy. Give yourself some slack. It seems to me the most important adjustment you need to make is to allow yourself the freedom to discover who you are, who you really are. That's what real freedom is, living apart from other people's expectations, apart from your own unrealistic expectations, finally being yourself and knowing without doubt that you are still loved and accepted."

Trevor walked to the logs, inspecting them by touch. He wasn't sure what to say. Perhaps he was just feeling sorry for himself. He always hated watching others dive deep into their own pity. He hoped once again that Zac was more understanding and sympathetic than he himself had ever been. Trevor tore off a small piece of bark and held it to his nose. It was Oak. He remained silent and felt the darkness closing in on him.

"Does any of this make sense to you?" Zac asked.

"I'm trying," Trevor said. "I really am. But the world you grew up in and the world I grew up in must have been very different. I know you like to talk about unconditional love, but when I look back to my childhood those words don't make any sense. I wonder about my dad. Could he ever have put my needs before his? I don't think he had the capacity. Could he love me based not on what I accomplished, but solely on me being me? I want to imagine it, more than you realize. I just can't. It's all too much like a fairy tale, a place that wasn't, and could never be. End of story."

"You could be right," Zac said. "You certainly have history on your side. But I think you're wrong. And I am curious how long it takes a man who has walked through a desert to quench his thirst. Sure, it could take hours, maybe even days to rehydrate, but the man doesn't stop drinking just because he has suffered. There is a thirst in you, in everyone, but probably more pronounced in you. You want love, real love. You want to be accepted. Unfortunately, you have no clear insight into what either of those words mean. You think you need to accomplish and achieve just so that someone will stop and say *there goes Trevor, he's quite a guy*, but they should have been saying that all along. And ever since the day you discovered the world did not offer what you needed, you set yourself on a mission to extract it anyway. You can't find gold in a coal mine. You cannot find what has always been missing in a world so full of brokenness and decay."

"Like I said, it's all about the two extremes we lived in."

"True," Zac said, "but now we share a world. I know you've been watching, but continue to keep your eyes open. Listen to the sounds and voices around you. Allow yourself to feel, not just at the tips of your fingers, but in your heart as well. As you travel through this valley during each of these remaining days, put little trust in where you've been, and even less in the direction you charted for yourself years ago. Remember there is more to learn."

"Is something going to happen?" Trevor asked, feeling concern again over his role in this adventure.

"Each day has enough trouble without bringing tomorrow into it," Zac said.

"My mom used to say that all the time when I was a kid," Trevor said, "but I assume you already know that. What you might not know is how much I hated hearing that. I still hate it."

The two men laughed and then succumbed to the stillness around them.

# 9

## Lost

Trevor wondered why he had not considered it before, that into each life some rain must fall. It was one of those ugly, gray, saturated mornings that make your bones feel heavy. He knew nothing of the local weather patterns or how often clouds rolled in, but in an environment as green as this it had to be often.

"Do you think that maybe we should just ride out the rain here in town?" Trevor asked. He knew rain would be bad enough, and it would only get worse if lightning started.

Zac pulled the nylon hood down off the top of his head. He looked up to the sky with a grin on his face, and then stuck out his tongue to catch a few drops.

"I've never understood why people are so afraid of water when it falls from the sky. It's okay to experience something different. When was the last time you walked in the rain?"

"I'm not sure, but this whole journey has been about something different, everyday."

"Good point," Zac said, and then began heading toward the edge of town. "So what makes you think you can't learn anything out here in the rain?" he called out over his shoulder.

Trevor lifted his face to the sky. He felt the rain land on his cheeks, collect there for a moment and then roll down his face and neck, eventually soaking into his shirt. There really was nothing to fear. It was an odd sensation, not one that he was used to, but it was just one more irrefutable reminder of how alive he was. Trevor licked his lips, lapping up the moisture around his mouth. He couldn't remember the last time he intentionally let himself get drenched in a rainstorm. He pulled his hood down in a show of respect and admiration for the man with whom he traveled, and then followed hard after Zac.

*Maybe I will learn something today.*

Not far out of town Zac stopped and pointed straight ahead. "The path heads that way, but I know another way we can go that will save us a few miles of hiking. It won't be easy, but it will be shorter."

"I'm in," Trevor said, barely giving it a thought. Having never backed down from a fight or challenge gave him all the currency he needed to be a little cocky. He often told himself he could do anything, and for a number of years he actually believed it. During the past decade, however, doubt began to creep in as minor failures started piling up. "I'm definitely in," he said once more, hoping this time to convince himself.

"Are you sure?" Zac asked. "It gets pretty rough in spots."

"If you can lead the way, I won't be far behind," Trevor said, and immediately wondered if he sounded as silly as he felt for making such a statement.

"I've been told I have a pretty good sense of direction," Zac said, veering off the trail and slipping through an opening between a pair of pine trees.

This section of the In-Between was much different than what

Trevor had experienced to this point. Everything seemed larger and wilder here. The trees stood taller and stronger, and the canopy did a fair job of filtering out some of the rain. There was no trail to follow, but there was an endless number of lichen covered rocks littering the forest floor. Some were no larger than a golf ball, others as big as a car. Those, along with fallen trees, soon made it clear there would be no straight line through this part of the forest. Far from being a hike, this was more like an exercise class. Knees high over shin high stones, hurdle a decaying tree trunk, shuffle left to avoid a large boulder, arms out in front to push back branches in the way. The two men were continually detouring and then realigning themselves with their invisible trail, only to repeat the process again and again.

As they walked, mud collected on their shoes so that each step became just a bit more drudgery than the one before it. This forced them to make occasional stops to clean their shoes, only to have their soles weighed down again in a matter of minutes. Progress seemed excruciatingly slow and Trevor wondered how such a difficult shortcut could save anyone time. He also grew concerned that Zac might become lost in such virgin terrain.

Within just a few hours, Trevor could feel the fatigue settling into his legs. The reality of his age and lack of fitness were coming into play again. His clothes were nearly soaked by the mixture of rain and sweat, and the only encouraging sight was the thinning clouds above. Trevor sensed the sun might break through at any moment.

"Did someone say this was the easy way?" Trevor asked.

"No," Zac replied, "I just said it would be shorter. Do you need a break?"

"I'm fine," Trevor pretended, certain that Zac could see through his act.

"Because I'd like to stop, if that's okay with you?" Zac asked. Trevor's knees immediately gave way and he dropped himself down upon a rock, relieved he could finally take a break. "Just up there by the river is a good spot," Zac continued, failing to notice that Trevor had already found a seat.

Trevor sat there momentarily, defiantly, refusing to follow. He was demoralized and watched Zac move on without him. Something seemed different today, this hike wasn't all about rainbows and lollipops. Trevor eventually picked himself up and started walking again, but his steps were slow and labored. After what seemed much further than it was, he broke from the thick and stood in a small patch of lush green grass near the bank of a small river. The water was running high and fast as one would expect in Spring. On the far side of the river stood a thin line of trees and beyond that a large field, smooth and level from what Trevor could see. Perhaps the worst was behind him.

Crossing the river might have been a challenge, were it not for the scores of rocks jutting out above the surface of the water. Twenty yards upstream, Trevor noticed the rocks thinned to nothing, and twenty yards downstream it was the same.

*Maybe Zac did know his way around these parts.*

They had managed to find the perfect and perhaps only spot from which to make a safe, dry crossing. The two men shared a fallen tree as their bench and rummaged through their packs for a snack.

"How much further 'til we get back on the trail?" Trevor

asked.

"We still have quite a way to go," Zac said, "but if we really push it I think we can make it by nightfall." This was not what Trevor wanted to hear. He sat as motionless as he could, stretching out legs that felt stiff and swollen, hoping they would somehow recover. The thought of hiking six or more hours kept him somber and quiet. He wanted desperately to admit to himself, as well as to Zac, that he couldn't go that far, but was afraid that both men might lose respect for him if he did.

Zac grabbed both water bottles and made his way to the edge of the river for a refill. He moved like a man with plenty of energy left, which only made Trevor feel worse.

They stayed there for the better part of an hour; Zac telling stories about some of the people he had met along his travels, and Trevor not wanting to interrupt for fear they might refocus on their journey. The stories Zac told seemed alien to Trevor. There was one about an amazing young man named Bob, and another about a kind hearted woman named Erika. There was Rick, and Natalie, and Trisha, and Mimi, each one interesting, bright, caring, funny, and so many other good things that it was making Trevor nauseous. It sounded too much like an obnoxious parent bragging about their children, children who really weren't all that special. The problem, clear to Trevor, was that each person Zac spoke about was being viewed through the distorted eyesight of an underly critical nature, so that each was placed on a pedestal where they didn't belong. Trevor listened politely, but inside he was far less tolerant. It was one of those days when everything seemed to irritate him, and if Zac was going to brag on anyone, then why not someone who deserved it?

When the time finally came, Zac led their way across the river taking care to choose stones both sturdy and dry. Trevor was surprised at how good he felt, thinking there might be a chance that he could keep up for the rest of the day.

Once on the other side, they cut through the tree line and into a vast clearing free of obstructions. This was ideal for Trevor, and when the sun finally broke through the clouds, he could feel his attitude lifting as well. They kept on, hiking comfortably through several large fields, but this was not to last. Before long they found themselves inside another forest, stepping high over stones, ankles stretched and tortured, thighs burning, moving slowly through an obstacle course that seemed, at least to Trevor, merciless. At one point the two men actually found themselves on all fours, scrambling over a hill covered with oversized rocks.

"Funny how they never mentioned this in the brochure," Zac said jokingly.

Trevor said nothing. His mood was dark. Just as in life when he lost touch, fixating on pain and the work required to get beyond it, he drew himself into a shell, detaching from everything and everyone around him. This was a reality that Trevor had known well, where only the strong survive—kill or be killed. Now he found himself at battle with a new world, and even though Zac tried several more times to start up a conversation, or lighten things up, it was no use, Trevor's focus could not be broken.

Evening arrived and Trevor wondered how much longer Zac

could or would continue. Trevor was exhausted beyond description, but the younger man had not lost a step all day. Trevor felt embarrassed to ask for a night's rest, but the light was failing and so was he. It was hard to understand that only a few short days ago Zac seemed very intentional about taking time to breathe, to relax, to soak it all in. None of that meant anything now. Trevor wondered why. He was skeptical about Zac's warning of coyotes and the need to get beyond the next river.

*There has to be more not being said. But what? Is there some unspoken deadline we're racing to meet? What is he hiding?*

Up until this point, time was not even an issue, so where was the sense in taking a shortcut when it didn't really matter how quickly they crossed the In-Between? Trevor held back his questions, but with each step his ire was growing. He also noticed that Zac had been conspicuously quiet, with little more than a sentence or two at only a handful of times during the day.

*Something is definitely wrong.*

Trevor stepped out of the forest and onto a riverbank. Darkness had washed away most of the daylight now. What Trevor's eyes saw was more about shapes and sizes than colors and details, registering slowly over tens of seconds. He hated to believe it, but it became impossible to deny. As he looked up the river all he could see, barely, was the surface of the water. He then looked down the river, and unless his sight had grown dramatically worse in an instant, there was nothing there but water as well. Straight ahead, however, was a different story. Just a few feet away, partially hidden by the approaching night, partially hidden by the river, were stones. The very same stones he relied on to cross this river hours earlier. Trevor quickly concluded that Zac had lost his way and they had traveled in a circle. The energy spent; wasted. The pain felt; fruitless. Trevor was livid. He hated waste, but what he hated even more was inconvenience. The idea of laboring for an entire afternoon with nothing to show for it was burning like a red coal in his mind, consuming the last of his patience. Without realizing it, one of Trevor's least endearing qualities was about to bubble over.

"I thought you knew where you were going," Trevor shouted, challenging Zac and his sense of direction.

"What are you talking about?" Zac asked. He could have unloaded as well, even he was tired now, yet he still found a way to avoid reaction.

"We were here before," Trevor ranted, waving his arms in a violent manner. "Don't you get it? You got lost. You took us in a big circle, and now, here we are, again."

Zac stared at Trevor. There was no fire in his eyes, only compassion. He wondered how far Trevor might go before checking himself. He hoped things wouldn't escalate, but he also knew better.

"I think you're wrong, but we'll know for sure when we get to the other side," Zac said.

"That's right, we will," Trevor scolded. "And then we'll know how many hours of our time you wasted."

"Trevor," Zac said calmly, "I didn't waste our time. Please don't get worked up about this."

"Don't ever tell me what to do," Trevor barked and then hurried onto the rocks. His steps were much faster than earlier in the day, almost frantic, moving recklessly from stone to stone. Worse still, the fatigue in his legs brought about a serious lack of coordination. Somewhere near the far side of the river he made a terrible mistake. His right foot found its way onto a large stone anchored to the river floor, but covered with water from the spit of gentle rapids. The foot slid off the rock and lodged securely between two in the riverbed. Unfortunately, Trevor's momentum could not be easily stopped. His body tipped forward, yawing helplessly, foot locked in position, until finally it felt as if the tissue in his ankle exploded. Fortunately, the foot slipped free before the bone broke, and by landing in a pool of frigid water, his knees and elbows were spared the pain of impact against the river floor. Trevor tried to regain his footing, but the pain that shot through his lower leg made it clear that this was a very bad idea.

Within seconds Zac was by his side lifting him from the water, protecting his damaged ankle, and helping him to the river's edge. Zac carefully lowered him to the ground.

"It's bad," Trevor said, still caught up in his anger. He was in great pain and grabbing for his ankle, hoping somehow he could stop the throbbing.

"I can help," Zac said with a determined look. He began to undo the lace of Trevor's hiking shoe. Trevor wasn't sure what to think and more than a bit concerned over what might be a poorly administered home remedy.

"No. Leave the shoe on," Trevor commanded, contorting his body as spikes of pain overtook him. "It keeps the swelling down."

Zac looked up from what he was doing, his face full of

concern. Trevor studied his eyes and noticed there was not even a glimmer of doubt. Then it happened again. Even though Zac was kneeling, he seemed larger and more full of conviction than Trevor had seen before.

"I need you to trust me," Zac said, and in that moment Trevor became a child again, trusting implicitly everything a parent might do to clean and patch a scrape. He was shocked at how easy it was to trust this man only moments after being so angry with him. He was also surprised at how confident Zac could be. The confidence to know that everything could be fine in the midst of a crisis. The confidence to say what he believed, without the fear of condemnation or rejection. The confidence to be exactly who he was in every situation. Nothing more. Nothing less. It was confidence such as this that made trust a simple matter.

Zac slowly and gently pulled away the cold, wet sock. Trevor could see how badly swollen the ankle was already. Zac carefully wrapped his hands around the ankle. He closed his eyes and Trevor imagined he saw Zac's lips moving.

What happened next left Trevor speechless. Initially he felt heat pouring into his leg, warm at first, but quickly ramping up near the point of discomfort. Pure energy streaming through skin, muscle, sinew and bone. And then, what felt like a quick burst of swelling. After that, just as quickly, the swelling was gone. Zac pulled his hands away after no more than half a minute, the ankle cooled, and everything felt normal again.

*How could it be normal?*

"I think you're good to go," Zac said.

"What?" Trevor asked. He recognized the pain was gone, but an injury such as this would take days or weeks to recover from.

"The ankle is whole," Zac replied. He said nothing more, waiting to see what Trevor would do.

It took a few seconds, but when the possibility of healing registered in Trevor's brain he pulled his leg close to his body and grabbed the ankle. It felt terribly right. Locked somewhere between disbelief and fear, he rolled to his side and placed his foot on the ground, testing it with only the weight of his leg. It was strong. He stood up, and like a man who has just dodged a head on car collision, Trevor was shaking with adrenalin.

*How could this be?*

The ankle was fine. It was better than fine, it was miraculous. A million thoughts danced through Trevor's head, but not a single one made it to his lips. He had seen some incredible things since arriving at the In-Between, but this was a complete betrayal of science and reason. Logic failed him, and he had put his faith in logic for so long. All the while Zac watched, a tutor studying his pupil, waiting for the next flurry of questions.

Trevor walked, one shoe on, one shoe off. He set off slowly at first, as cautiously as he could, worried that each step might reinjure the ankle. He cut through the tree line and into the field beyond, faster and faster, gaining confidence with each step, until eventually he was running at full speed. He kept this up for longer than he thought possible, gradually lifting his line of sight to the horizon as he felt more secure in the strength of his ankle. Suddenly he stopped, feeling disheartened and gasping for air. In the distance, painted against a dark blue sky which held the final traces of light, Trevor could see the silhouette of a large solitary tree. It was at that moment he realized this was a different field than the one he traveled earlier in the day, and behind him ran a different river.

# 10

# The Confession

By the time Trevor made his way back to the river, Zac had already set up camp. The bed rolls were in place and a fire was raging. Trevor stood at the edge of the tree line watching Zac collect firewood. The smaller limbs he broke over his knee, the thicker ones he snapped with his foot. Regardless of how big or small each piece was, Zac appeared as nothing more than an average guy spending time in the wilderness. Trevor took a few steps closer and Zac looked over.

"Everything okay?" Zac asked

Trevor nodded his head and sat down on the ground near the fire. His senses were operating in overdrive and he was amazed at how fresh everything felt. He could hear the soft rush of wind blowing through leaves and the crackle of burning wood. The firelight danced on nearby trees, and beyond that, a moon close to full created shadows in the night. Trevor's nose was filled with the scent of smoke and ash, while his body, at times, was beaten back by the heat of the flame. It was an orchestra of sensations, some subtle, others strong, working together to create an unforgettable symphony. On most nights it would have been the perfect ending to a difficult day. Tonight Trevor needed answers, some insight to connect what he knew with what he didn't.

"I have to ask you something," Trevor said.

"I guess it's about time," Zac acknowledged and stared into Trevor's eyes as if measuring the depth of his soul. Trevor hesitated long enough to collect his determination.

"What just happened?" he asked.

"Are you sure you're ready for the truth?"

"I certainly don't want to believe a lie any longer," Trevor said. Zac was unable to hold back a smile at the wisdom of such words.

"Understood, but I need to start with a few questions of my own," Zac said. He walked to his pack and took a long sip from his water bottle. At first this seemed innocuous, but then Trevor wondered if he might be in for more than he bargained, if Zac was preparing for a long and arduous speech. Zac then innocently tossed Trevor's missing shoe and sock to him.

"When you walked the earth, did you ever think there was life after death?" Zac asked.

"No," Trevor said while replacing his sock, "it didn't make any sense. I think I had science on my side."

"Perhaps, but would you agree you were wrong about that?" Zac asked.

Trevor nodded reluctantly.

"Good. How about relationships? Would you say you were successful figuring out the relational side of life?"

Trevor wasn't real happy with this game, but if he expected honesty then maybe he needed to give as well as he got. "I think there were a lot of things I could have done better," Trevor conceded.

"And what about the quality of your life?" Zac asked. "Were you able to find much joy and peace, or was it mostly about survival?"

"We've already talked about that," Trevor said.

"Yes we did. And now I'm guessing it would be fair to say that you are very much like the seven billion people you left behind on that planet you called home," Zac said. "Human, fallible—sometimes right, sometimes wrong."

"I think that's fair," Trevor said.

"Excellent. Sometimes when we get to a place of humility, a place of weakness, we can find tremendous strength," Zac said. "When you get to the place where you accept human frailty, great things can happen. Are you ready to experience greatness?"

Trevor was uncomfortable. He was the type of person who preferred to be driving an interrogation instead of buckling under the weight of one. He simply wanted to know what force it was that brought him to the In-Between, shook the foundation of several long held beliefs, and then finally brought healing to a badly damaged leg. Zac had been a good friend since they met, but it was hard to understand what made him tick. Trevor only wanted a few simple answers and was now afraid of where those answers might lead.

Trevor took his eyes off Zac and stared into the fire. He watched the tips of the flame jump and fall repeatedly, and then realized how little he knew of fire. "I just want to understand," he said softly.

Zac walked close and placed a hand on Trevor's shoulder.

"And you will." He picked up a few limbs and threw them on the fire, taking a few more seconds to stoke the flame. Trevor felt the pressure inside growing and wasn't sure how much longer he could wait. He looked up again. Zac's face, lit by the firelight, was different now. It appeared weather worn, as if he had passed this way hundreds of times, carrying stories of ages past like some ancient sage. Zac drew a deep breath and began.

"Did you ever look up at the night sky, at the thousands of stars your eyes can see, knowing there are billions beyond your sight? And as your mind struggles to grasp the vastness of space, a nagging question forms in the depths of your brain—where did it all come from? Cosmologists like to talk about the Big Bang and the conservation of mass-energy, but they fail to address the basic question of a child. Where did it all come from? How can anything come from nothing?

"Biologists take a different approach; they investigate the intricacies of the human body. Starting with limbs and organs, they narrow their field of vision by trying to understand the function of more specialized tissues, muscle, bone, and tendon. But they can't stop there, refusing to let the mystery go unsolved. Molecules, proteins, genomes—each telling the story of a brilliant complexity which humans have already spent millions of man years trying to comprehend. Still it eludes them.

"And what of the mind? Less than five pounds of soft tissue that is fueled by electric pulses to stimulate something the world's most powerful computers fail to achieve; imagination. If we know little of the body, we know nothing of the mind, and yet it drives and

110

directs us through 70, 80, 90 years of living. It can take a poor man living on the street and make him feel like he has everything, or a rich man with millions and convince him he has nothing. Is there anything as fascinating, or as baffling, as the mind?"

Trevor remained quiet. He was nervous now and busied himself by rubbing his hands across pants that were still damp from the river, but his ears and mind remained as focused as they had ever been. His gaze moved from place to place, but never directly at his friend. Zac continued.

"It's an accident some tell us. The random collisions and interactions of atoms, molecules, and energy. The slow and steady evolution from lifeless dirt to the rods and cones of the human eye. I, for one, have a hard time accepting that all this order and precision is merely the result of rolling dice. Everything I see cries out that there must be a creator, a master designer who intricately weaves life in the most beautiful and surprising ways.

"But people are born into a world of pain and sorrow. People like yourself. People who learn hard lessons before the promise of a better life can be awakened, before the hope of eternity congeals and a better path discovered. It forms scales upon their eyes and distorts their hearing. It separates them from much of their potential, and drives them to a parched and barren land where they don't belong. A piece of them dies, and then another, and another. And somewhere, unknown to most, a father cries for his children."

At that moment Trevor looked up. Whether it was the reference to a father that Trevor never felt he had, or the slowing cadence of speech causing him to expect a conclusion, his eyes met

Zac's and he immediately lost the will to turn them away.

"Trevor, as sure as I stand before you, there is a God. The God. The One who breathes life into the great blue whale, the smallest microorganism, and the man who rejects Him. He hangs the stars, spins the electron, and is the driving force for everything between the two. He exists throughout time as if it weren't there. He always was. He always will be. The mind works to keep pace, but it's futile. He transcends. He is. And as much as you may try and push Him to the deep recesses of nothingness, He exists apart from you and beyond you. You breathe because of Him. You think because of Him. You exist because of Him. You owe Him everything, and He asks nothing.

"This whole place, the land in which you have walked these past few days, is just another sliver of His creation. It exists because some people, like yourself, could not see the truth while they roamed the Earth. It exists because God, the very one that created you, desired a way to have fellowship with you, even though you turned from Him. It exists to set things right, the way they should have always been. It is a second chance, a new beginning, salvation.

"Every day since your life began, He has pursued you. Now, after your death, He continues that pursuit. His love is ageless, reckless, limitless, and relentless.

"Your leg was badly damaged, that is true, but what challenge is it to heal an ankle for the God who birthed a billion galaxies? Is it any different than the simple act of painting a beautiful sunset, or bringing a smile to your face? It is, as always, Him reaching out to you in order to make your life more whole, more complete."

Zac stopped. His words had been carefully crafted to penetrate a parched soul, much the way water changes the consistency of a dry sponge. Trevor sat, quiet and stunned. Forty years of living under a single belief system can be a difficult shackle to break free from. There had been many lessons along this journey that Trevor appreciated learning, hard as they were, but this was one he felt he could have done without. He rose to his feet, not wanting to feel more vulnerable than he already was.

"So are you telling me that you are God?" Trevor asked.

"Yes and no," Zac responded.

Trevor rubbed his forehead. "Which is it?"

"I have many names," Zac said. "Some call me the stone which the builders rejected, because there was no place for me in your world. Others have called me the cornerstone, because without me, nothing could be built. I am known as the shepherd, gathering his sheep and watching over them. Sometimes they just refer to me as the carpenter. I am the vine, for those who have found life have found it in me. I am the lamb who has been sacrificed so that all may know God, the lion who returns in victory. I am the teacher, the healer, the deliverer. I am His son. His only son. I am in Him, and He is in me. But you may know me by another name—Jesus."

"This doesn't make sense," Trevor protested.

"Maybe it does," Zac said. "Maybe all that you held to, your beliefs, your religion, was really just a lie, a deception. Have you considered that?"

"Let me get this straight," Trevor said, "you want me to believe that you are the guy that walked the Earth—that some people say walked the Earth—two thousand years ago?"

"Don't you know it already?" Zac asked. "Isn't there something inside telling you it has to be so, or are you still trying to shut down that part of yourself, trying desperately to control that which you have no control over?"

Trevor turned his head and stared into the emptiness of the night. He was numb. Clarity of thought was now replaced by a gray and somber haze. After moments of wrestling with the unthinkable, he looked toward Zac.

"Listen, I can admit I have seen some amazing things since we met," Trevor said, "but if you are who you claim to be, where were you in life? Where were you when my mom struggled to put food on the table, when I fought to make a name for myself? Where was your friendship when I really needed it?"

"I was there," Zac replied. "Your sixth grade teacher would have done anything she could to help, but you wanted none of it. And what about Mr. Krueger down the street? Didn't you notice something different about him? Couldn't you see people were trying to reach you, that I was trying to reach you? You just wouldn't let me in."

"Certainly the God of the universe could have found a way into my life," Trevor said. "It was for my own good."

"Please try to understand," Zac said, "because it can be very difficult to grasp the ways of the infinite with a finite mind. God's love has been given to you. It is a gift, and not many people understand what that word means. Most of us give gifts so that we can receive things in return, but God gives gifts because He loves us, because He truly and unconditionally loves us. Whether you accept or reject Him, His love remains a constant. Try wrapping your head around that idea. You can despise Him with every fiber of your being and He will refuse to love you any less. Yet there can be an ocean of difference between what God demands and what God desires. He demands nothing from you, but He desires everything. He wants your love, your friendship, your trust, your adoration. He wants to be your father, and you to be His son, and He wants that into, and throughout, eternity. He will not coerce you to do anything. Besides, if I forced my way into your life how would you have responded? I walked the earth for 33 years, performed miracles in front of thousands, and still people refused to believe. It takes two to establish a relationship, but only one to keep it from happening."

"It just seems like there must have been something you could have done," Trevor said with disappointment. And with that Trevor turned and walked alone into the field, into the darkness. He wanted to think. He wanted to be by himself. Once again, Trevor reverted to the only equation for coping he had ever known—seizing absolute control of a situation and working things over and over in his mind until a practical solution or viable option presented itself. This had always been his greatest strength. It continued to be his greatest weakness.

# 11

# Acceptance

Trevor walked along the edge of a field that was held gray by the power of the night. He could see a stark contrast between the darkness of the woods to his right and the moonlit grassland to his left, and he kept near the border of the two. He held close to the tree line, hoping to experience the fear and excitement of being near the unknown, but not so close that he wouldn't see an animal if one were to attack. He told himself his chosen course had nothing to do with the large tree in the center of the field, but he also knew that he was still willing to lie to himself when it was convenient. Trevor hated that tree—a nagging reminder that Zac had been right and he had been wrong.

His clothes were still damp and provided far more discomfort than he wanted, especially now that the night air was cooling. Trevor missed the warmth and light of the fire, but it was best that he was on his own right now. He suddenly realized that to this point in his journey he had done nothing apart from Zac. An adventurous piece of his soul stirred. He took a deep breath and exhaled for all the world to hear. Perhaps this was his opportunity to head back into the mountains to explore. Maybe he should follow the river across the valley and into a town that he could call home. Trevor recalled that there were no rules here. He could do anything he wanted, unless of course Zac was deceiving him about that as well. He unknowingly looked to his left. The large tree stood in the center of the field, as if watching Trevor from afar. His anger grew.

Trevor's ankle caught on a stick. It held tight for a second—long enough for him to lose his balance—and then let go with just enough time for Trevor to bring his foot forward and prevent a fall. His foot slammed down hard on the ground. His ankle was still fine. He turned and reached, picking up the stick and then breaking it to pieces. He threw each piece into the woods, one after the other, hoping that something, anything, might happen.

*Am I really that helpless, traveling a path I don't even get to choose? Are there really unseen forces directing my movements and influencing my decisions? Am I that unaware? What's the point? Why would a god, or the God, go to such trouble?*

Trevor wondered if at this very moment his thoughts were in fact his own, or just the clever manipulation of a superior being. He turned and stared defiantly in the direction of the tree. His body stiffened, as did his resolve.

*I will never be a puppet.*

He continued walking the perimeter of the field, only this time somewhat faster than before. He started thinking about his options—where he might go, what he might see, and what was left to accomplish apart from this so-called God he had recently become aware of. Trevor needed ideas to help him escape from a reality he refused to accept. He let his mind run free.

While his steps bent back the soft grass of the field, thoughts of his past began creeping into his brain. Like a tiny child gently knocking on a thick wooden door, the thoughts kept up, almost imperceptibly, until Trevor could hold them back no more. He found himself replaying scenes from his childhood, one of the many forms of mental anguish Trevor often subjected himself to. Although he had the ability to recall his past with amazing clarity, it was usually just another chance to chastise himself for poor decisions, missed opportunities, and a failure to make discerning judgments.

Trevor remained lost in thought for some time. When he finally lifted his eyes from the field, he found himself precisely where he did not want to be. He had wandered to the base of the tree. As if guided by a hidden magnet, his steps bent along a strange course toward the center of the field.

The tree was larger than he had judged from the edge of the clearing, and also more inviting. Trees were part of his comfort zone growing up and he always found time to climb his way to one specific notch in his favorite maple to stand alone in his personal fortress. He enjoyed the opportunity to look down upon a world that was so much less than what it should have been.

Trevor circled slowly around the base of the tree searching for a branch from which to start his climb, but each limb looked to be just a little beyond his grasp. He eventually chose one and jumped as high as he could, leaning his body to one side so that the opposite arm could extend a little further. His fingers wrapped around the limb momentarily, then ripped loose when his body started falling toward the ground. He took a few steps back, ran forward and then jumped again. His hand reached, caught hold, gave somewhat to the weight of his body, but managed to hold on. He grabbed the limb with his other hand, lifted and wrapped his legs around, and awkwardly pushed and pulled his way to a standing position. He proceeded to climb, keeping close to the trunk, ignoring the growing distance between himself and the ground below.

At some point he sensed an unnatural clearing in the canopy overhead. He climbed further and realized there was a small wooden platform built to one side. Trevor scrambled onto the platform, sitting carefully with his legs hanging off the side. He scanned the field lit softly by moonlight and witnessed nothingness. The grass was still, time seemed meaningless, and his mind rewound back to his youth once more. He wondered how many stories he could recollect if he tried.

Trevor heard the soft rush of wings overhead and looked up to see a shadow of birds darting across the night sky. He imagined what it must feel like to be free, and continued watching them long after they disappeared into the darkness. Freedom. Why had it escaped him? Why was there always someone in charge with an agenda counter to his own? Parents. Bosses. Teachers. For as long as he could remember there was someone holding him back or slowing him down, someone like Zac, manipulating the playing field so that it was seldom, if ever, Trevor could come out on top.

*How could there possibly be a God? There is far too much pain in the world. Murder. Rape. War and greed. There is no justice, no harmony, no peace.*

Trevor stared at the gray below him, and clenched his teeth as his soul hardened. Everything made more sense now. Trevor was willing to accept the existence of a god, but this was an all controlling and vindictive god, with very little sense of equity. Too many had died. Too many had suffered. The good were struck down as evil triumphed.

*All he had to do was to let me know he was there. He wasn't really trying. He couldn't have been. I was alone, completely alone. He may control the universe, but he will never control me.*

Trevor looked toward the river and could still see the light of the fire bouncing off the surrounding trees. Maybe it was time to fight back, time to stand up against an unjust authority and battle for what was right and fair. He knew too well that power corrupts, and had learned hard lessons that those in power were selfish, with an eye bent on serving themselves. This storyline had played itself out a countless number of times in the pages of history, and in Trevor's life.

He laid his back against the wooden platform and stared into the night sky wondering what he should do. As he did, exhaustion took hold of him. He realized even he could think no more. He slid his body further onto the planks, gave no thought to the danger of rolling off in the middle of the night, and closed his eyes, content that morning was a better time to make decisions.

# 12

# Rebellion

Trevor was up, throwing a few loose items into his pack. He didn't care if Zac woke. He didn't care if he slept. Either way Trevor's mind was set. He knew what had to be done.

"What's going on?" Zac asked, rubbing his head as if that might brush away the fatigue.

"Don't worry about it," Trevor said, being as short as he could be.

Zac sat up in his bed roll. He understood what was happening. "Can we talk this out?"

"I don't think so," Trevor said, throwing the pack on his shoulder. "I think I heard enough last night." He took a few steps toward the river.

"Where will you go?" Zac asked.

"Somewhere better than this," Trevor said. He made his way carefully across the river and back into the forest, retracing his steps from the day before. Zac laid back and stared at the sky, exhaling a chest full of air, old and stale. A few minutes passed before Zac heard the familiar cracking of sticks underfoot. Trevor worked his way back to the far side of the river.

"I do have one question for you," Trevor called out.

"Go ahead." Zac felt bad for Trevor and recognized the

squall that he was caught up in, but he also knew that storms were often necessary to shake dead wood from a tree. The behavior was far more predictable than Trevor could have realized.

"I find it hard to believe that the God of the universe (isn't that what you called yourself?) would hide behind the body of a diminutive mountain man. Why not just tell me who you were from the beginning? It doesn't sound all that god-like to me." Trevor stood with muscles tightened, chest swollen in defiance, expecting a weak and timid explanation that he could easily disregard.

Zac pulled back the top cover from his legs. His movements were relaxed, but heightened Trevor's anxiety. Zac stood, slowly and intentionally. For a moment it appeared that his legs were pushing down earth, instead of merely lifting his torso. He didn't look as diminutive as Trevor remembered, and he also seemed far more intimidating. He fixed his eyes on Trevor, not with anger, but with purpose. Trevor found it difficult to maintain eye contact. Zac began speaking and his voice filled Trevor's ears, rising above the sounds of the river and the forest.

"Everything I have done, everything, has been with you in mind, in your best interest. As you felt hunger, pain, confusion or loneliness, brought on by your hand or the hand of others, I used it to teach, to build, to help you grow. You seldom saw it that way, and in that you are not alone, because few encounter struggle and recognize its value.

"What I offer you, what I offer everyone, is the hardest and easiest path a man can travel. Easy, because I place very little burden upon my people—my yoke is light. Hard, because it cuts across

122

everything the world has taught you–my ways are not man's ways.

"I know you need to go. I've known it all along. But as you go be certain that you understand one thing, you are loved in ways you cannot even fathom, and that love is timeless."

Trevor paused for longer than he wanted. Zac's words were more than he expected. Why couldn't he respond with a whimper, or better yet, with anger and judgment? That Trevor could understand. That he could fight. But responding to rejection with love didn't make any sense, and now there seemed no good way to strike back. Trevor thought for a few seconds about the integrity of the man with whom he battled, and the unmistakable imprint made on Trevor's after life, but the wheels of rebellion were too long in motion and Trevor felt little need to slow them now.

"Fraud," Trevor said quietly, and walked away.

The plow bit the earth, creating a small wave of dirt that rolled up out of the shallow opening and then crashed upon the surface. The field was full of such tracings, but Trevor still found it difficult to hold a straight line. He clenched tightly with both hands, arms taut, but no matter how hard he tried the plow seemed to have a will of its own. Straight lines were best, that much he knew, but the plow chose differently. It cut sharply to the right here or gradually slid left there. "Why was it so hard to stay on course?" he wondered.

With a bit more practice, more time spent wrestling the plow, Trevor was confident he would be able to straighten his lines. He knew the fire in his belly was what made men great. It separated those willing to work harder from those who were lazy and weak, those who would sacrifice from those afraid of risk, those who reach for glory from those who settle for so much less. Periodically, he pulled the two horse team to a stop in order to survey his work. It had only been a couple of days but he was already improving, and although the field didn't look like much yet, it was easy to imagine the sea of growth that would rise up in a few weeks time.

The work was hard, extremely demanding, but he understood all that before he signed on with Jacob and Jeremy. Trevor recognized there had to have been something in their lives that forged these brothers into men of steel, and he was now trying to follow in their footsteps. He woke each morning just before sunrise, inhaled a quick breakfast, and then went straight to the field. There he labored like a beast, breaking only 15 or 20 minutes for lunch. He gave everything he had, fully exhausting both muscle and joint, hands blistered and raw at the end of each day. The labor ended near sunset with just enough time to squeeze in a dinner before he finally collapsed. It was a difficult burden, but this was what Trevor loved most, pushing and driving himself in ways almost heartless. It somehow brought him joy.

And so it seemed that through a strange journey filled with turns and detours, Trevor had found his home. This was an eternity that suited him. One that he could appreciate. This was where he longed to be, where he felt most comfortable, and no man could have prepared more during the course of a lifetime than he.

He reached the end of the field, called out a few instructions to the horses while pulling the reigns hard to the right. He lifted and reset the plow in the opposite direction, and then removed his right hand from the handle just long enough to see it was bleeding again. He felt proud that this could not slow him, proud that he was invincible. At that moment Trevor wondered why it had been so difficult for others to understand him. Why even his own wife failed to comprehend the man with whom she shared a life? Was it such an immense task to recognize that some men are driven? That some men fix their eyes on goals and ambitions, and whether they achieve or not, grow to appreciate the struggle under which they labor.

It was late in the day now and the thought of dinner was slowly overtaking Trevor's mind. Perhaps the brothers had forgotten him tonight. His body was tired, his hunger growing, and as he glanced to the horizon to recalculate the time of day, something out of the ordinary caught his attention.

The sun had nearly dropped behind the mountains, and being so low in the sky it forced his eyes to squint. Someone was out there, alone, walking the edge of the field near the trees. The way he moved and the manner in which he carried himself left no doubt in Trevor's mind. It was Zac.

Trevor leaned the plow to the ground and began walking toward the perimeter, surprised at how badly he wanted to see his friend. Zac stopped and waited.

Trevor's mind rewound to the other day. The cruel words. The cold stare. He hadn't meant any of it, or if he did, he desperately wanted those moments back now. He hoped, believed, and knew that Zac would forgive him. In only a few short days Zac had become a great friend, hardly deserving the harsh treatment Trevor dealt him.

*But how could it be true? Jesus?*

That was still problematic.

*Why would a god, or even a man, spend time with someone who could not have thought or cared less about him? Why, with all the people out there trying to get his attention, would he dedicate so much effort to make himself known to a man of doubt or blatant disbelief? And why was he so damn easy to get along with? So caring? So sincere? So complete?*

As the distance between the two narrowed to tens of feet, Trevor could feel excitement rising up inside. He stepped carefully, avoiding the ruts he cut earlier in the day. Trevor genuinely longed to see Zac, and for the first time he wondered if it could have been Zac that was responsible for leading him to this last stop along his journey. Perhaps Zac's cunning and calculated words were what drove Trevor to a place he could finally call home.

*Isn't that what gods were for?*

"I owe you an apology," Trevor said as he stood before Zac. He held out a dirt laden hand in friendship, and was surprised again at the strength in Zac's hand.

"It's okay," Zac said. "It had been a long day for both of us."

Trevor smiled because he could feel it again–Zac's way. That soft, gentle, unrelenting force always acting to make another feel at ease. It moved like fresh spring air after a rainstorm in June. In that instant Trevor realized their relationship had not been poisoned after all.

"What will you do now?" Zac asked.

Trevor looked back across the field of brown, hoping Zac would appreciate his masterpiece. "I'll get up each day and work the land," Trevor said. "I want to thank you for bringing me here. This is a good place for me. It's what I was designed for."

"No. Not at all," Zac said with conviction. "I was there the day my Father laid out a plan for your life. He didn't want you slaving away under a weight that was always too much to bear. He wanted you to breathe, to laugh, to smile, to experience joy, His joy, as if He was with you. It was magnificent. There was intimacy, curiosity, and prosperity—although a little different than what you might imagine —excitement, spice, fascination, and a newness that could barely be described. But you settled for something less in a fallen world. I understand why you made those compromises when you were eleven years old, and why you held to them for so long. I understand because you had no frame of reference. You hadn't been taught the lessons that were needed to make better decisions, decisions that would put you on a better road toward your destiny. That all makes sense to me. I just don't understand what you are doing now. This time around you've actually tasted it. You've seen glimpses of what eternity could be, and still you turn away. Please don't make this mistake twice."

"You didn't bring me here?" Trevor asked.

"Of course not," Zac said. "I want you with me. We still have a journey to complete, more to learn."

"Hey Trevor," a voice called. "Dinner time." It was Jacob. He was removing the harness from the horses, a chore that Trevor immediately felt guilt for not completing. Trevor grew restless. He hated allowing someone else to finish his work, especially someone as critical as Jacob.

"I still think I am in a pretty good place," Trevor said.

"I think you're being deceived," Zac said.

"Are you coming?" Jacob called.

Trevor was torn. He hadn't meant to leave things like this. It had been his intention to smooth things over with Zac, but now he wondered if he had only made them worse.

"I'm sorry," Trevor said. "Thank you for showing me this place. I like it here."

Zac stood still, watching his friend walk away, a friend still somewhat oblivious to how deeply he was cared for and by whom.

# 13

# Reconciliation

Trevor's eyes opened to darkness. Within seconds he was far more awake than he wanted, but still too tired to get out of bed. This all too familiar dance between sleep and consciousness had played itself out nearly every night for the last five years, and it somehow followed him to the In-Between. It kept him in a continual state of mild exhaustion, partially foggy and always slightly off his game. It was torture.

There were three things that filled the sleepless hours of his mind; regret over yesterday, disappointment for today, and worry for tomorrow—a racetrack of destructive thought that paralyzed and deceived. He should have left these battles behind a lifetime ago, but his brain refused to stop churning. It was barely more than a week since he traded a life of contentment for the hopelessness of his present situation. Inside he wanted to cry.

*Could I have been a bigger fool?*

Trevor lay on his back, unable to position his legs in a manner that allowed him to completely relax. He felt an unnatural pressure on his knees and hips as if they were bending in the wrong direction. As much as he tried not to, he kept focusing on the pain, slight as it was, remembering the days when there were no obstacles to sleep. It was hard to rest while in this position. Harder still to turn off his mind.

*Why wasn't I able to recognize a better life when it finally came my way? Why was I so stubborn?*

Trevor rolled to his left side, hoping to find a cure for his ailment. His head tilted in an odd fashion putting an uncomfortable strain on his neck. The pillow was too small but there was no point in asking his hosts for another, they had little concern for him. He was nothing more than a living machine that put a little more food on their table at the price of some floor space and dirty dishes. Zac, on the other hand, had always shown genuine concern and appreciation for all those who crossed his path. He gave freely of himself to anyone, whether in need or not. Trevor admired that trait of Zac's as much as any other, and even recognized a hint of jealousy, having never been able to step outside of himself and show such unselfish love to another.

*He really did try to reach me. I remember Mr. Krueger, all those times he offered to help me with my car, the times he tried to start up a conversation. I wouldn't let him in. I kept the door shut. It wasn't him. It was me.*

Turning on his stomach he found comfort, but he also knew it was only temporary. Before long his lower back would begin to ache, slight at first, but eventually unbearable. Trevor knew this drill too well, always hoping each night would be different, and still sleep eluded him.

*There should be more rest for someone so completely spent. I can't keep doing this.*

His mind continued pushing ahead. There was still so much to do. Weeds were already starting to grow and many acres remained

130

untouched by the plow. How could he possibly get it all done? He twisted onto his right side. More neck pain, shoulder pain, and frustration.

*What if it rains? What then?*

On and on, this conflict gripped him through the early hours of the morning. He could find no release. At some point he saw light streaming in from under the door. He heard steps in the kitchen and the muffled sound of men talking. The night had been far too short, provided too little rest, and it would soon be over.

The door swung open and a voice barked, "Get up lazy, we have work to do."

He didn't know if it was Jacob or Jeremy speaking. It didn't matter. They both seemed to dislike him. Trevor wondered if they might be more accepting if he worked harder, but what more could he do? The brothers worked a frenetic pace, far beyond what Trevor was accustomed to, and anyone not meeting quota was deemed a liability; a failure. Trevor's body was wearing down. His mind and emotions had bottomed out. He was, in every sense of the word, a broken man.

*How did I let myself accept a life so dim?*

He had been involved in the adventure of a lifetime, the adventure of two lifetimes, only to let it slip through his fingers in exchange for more time on the treadmill. Had the promise of a richer life been taken from him it would have been hard enough to bear, but to know that he gave it away of his own volition made his anguish worse.

The light of day was still growing when Trevor reached a field mostly covered by the shadow of the mountains. The hoe in his hand felt heavier than it was, a dividend of his emotional burden. He settled in to a furrow he dug earlier in the week and began chopping at nearby weeds.

After a few minutes, he started singing quietly, almost inaudibly, a song he barely knew. "Amazing grace, how sweet the sound, that saved a wretch like me." He hummed to fill in for the words that escaped him, and then continued. "Amazing grace, how sweet the sound, that saved a wretch like me." This simple ritual could go on for hours. Days earlier he found that work moved quicker and easier if he lost himself in song, he just wasn't sure why he chose this particular song.

But today things were different. Today it wasn't about filling time or occupying his mind. This was worship, and it felt good to admit that to himself. Trevor was finally coming to terms with God, himself, and the relationship between the two. This awakening was both wonderful and horrific. Horrific because after all this time, Trevor now had the capacity to acknowledge he truly was a wretch. But Zac had taught greater lessons than this along their journey, foremost, the unconditional love of a God whose forgiveness was always real and complete. Trevor now felt assured of that love, certain it would never fade. He also gained a better understanding of confidence, finding himself reliant on a strength much greater than his own.

In the distance Trevor could make out a familiar shape, a man, alone, walking in the shallow light just as he had every morning and evening for the past five days. Trevor recognized Zac and knew immediately what he had to do. Unfortunately, the two brothers had followed him into the field this morning and that would make things more complicated.

"I'm sorry," Trevor called to Jeremy, "I made a mistake." With that, he dropped his hoe to the ground and began walking toward Zac. In the distance Zac seemed aware of what was happening. He stopped and turned, holding his position at the edge of the field.

The brothers began laughing and then mocking Trevor's words. Trevor kept moving. He turned quickly when he heard footsteps racing toward him, but it was too late. Jeremy drove his shoulder into Trevor's ribs and brought him to the ground. Jeremy rose to his feet again. Trevor tried to follow, but a fist struck him on the cheekbone and dropped him back to the soil. He lay there for a moment in pain and disbelief. Trevor had finally caught a vision of Hell and wondered if he was too late to escape it.

"You don't just come and go as you please," Jeremy shouted over him. His eyes were full of venom and his fists were held tight. He started laughing when he heard his brother doing the same. Jacob was now standing over Trevor as well, and drove a boot into his side. Trevor winced, feeling more defeated than he wanted to remember.

"Leave him alone," Zac commanded. The brothers, surprised, took a step back as Zac moved in to help Trevor to his feet. Everyone seemed dumbfounded except for Zac. Trevor tried his best to right himself, but remained somewhat hunched over from pain. Zac and Trevor began slowly walking away.

"Hey," Jacob shouted, "you're not going anywhere." He

started walking toward Trevor, but Zac let go of his friend and stood as a barrier between the two. The larger man cast quite a shadow over Zac.

"You want some of this too?" Jacob asked, still hustling forward and then delivering a crushing blow to Zac's face that sent him backwards to the ground. Trevor leaned to help him up.

"Just go," Zac said, struggling to his feet with blood pouring from his nose. Trevor wasn't sure what to do. He continued walking. Zac tried to follow but the brother's weren't done yet. One of them swung a hoe against the back of Zac's knees. He fell to the ground and then quickly got up on all fours, only to have a leather boot land hard against his stomach. Trevor kept moving as he was told, with the sound of brutality and laughter fading behind him.

Eventually the brothers lost interest in Zac and he was allowed to leave. Trevor watched from a safe distance, and although Zac still appeared strong and determined, there was obvious pain in his stride. Trevor paid no attention to the brothers, and so he was unable to warn Zac as a rock, about the size of a brick, came hurtling toward him. It struck the right side of his back, near the shoulder blade, dropping him to his knees. Zac hunched over, hands on his thighs, as he dealt quietly with the pain.

In the distance, Jeremy held his hands above his head and yelled, "Yes."

Trevor hurried toward him. He could already see the blood soaking through Zac's torn shirt. He knelt down alongside Zac, wishing desperately there was something he could do to share in the pain that he helped bring about.

"I am so sorry," Trevor said. "I should have never come here. I don't know why I act like such a stubborn fool."

Zac looked up and managed a smile through his pain. "This journey was never about where you have been," Zac said, "it's always been about where you are going."

This time they would take the trail away from Smithfield. It was a longer trip, but each man had faced enough challenges in the recent past and the idea of light hiking sat well with both of them. It was safe now and Trevor knew he was in a much better place, both geographically and psychologically, but their physical wounds needed to be cleaned as best they could. They stopped near a stream and as Zac filled his water bottle, Trevor realized another consequence of his actions—his backpack had been left behind. They now had less food, less clothing, and one less bed roll for the night.

And then something wonderful took place. Trevor's normal reaction to an errant action or decision in the past, further from his reach than the stars in the sky, would be self-torment. This time he chose a different course, basking in a deep well of grace, and in those waters he discovered new motivation; to do better. Today, tomorrow, and every day afterward, he wanted to think the best thoughts he could, make the best choices he could, and walk the best path he could. If he strayed, so be it, because there would always be tomorrow, and with it a fresh opportunity to improve again. Less consumed with his own failure, Trevor's thinking quickly shifted beyond himself, in a new direction.

"We need to get your shoulder cleaned up," Trevor said,

walking to the stream. Zac said nothing. Trevor took the torn shirt in his hands and carefully ripped it away from Zac's wound. Then, deeply moved by something he failed to discern up to this point, Trevor stopped. His finger ran slowly along one of the many deep scars cut into the muscle of Zac's back. Trevor's eyes began to water.

"You died for us," Trevor said. "You really did."

Zac turned to him and said, "I died for you." Zac lifted his forearms. There, on each wrist, a deep scar remained, rough and discolored.

Trevor was speechless. He kept his head down as he considered what it meant to die on a cross. To hang on a tree while those nearby laugh and ridicule. To feel the loneliness and separation from everyone and everything. To sense time practically stop as each second brings new heights of suffering. To writhe in pain so intense that death becomes solace. To sacrifice yourself to save the very men, women, and children who despise your existence.

"I didn't deserve it," Trevor confessed.

"That thought never crossed my mind," Zac said.

A tear rolled down Trevor's cheek. He would never be the same.

# 14

# Healing

The land Trevor and Zac were passing through seemed to possess an untamed nature. Unlike the farmland left behind, there was far less evidence that this land had been shaped by the hands of men. With the exception of the narrow dirt trail they traveled, this landscape might have been the same since time began. It was near primeval and felt perfect in its wildness.

Not long ago, it would have been nearly impossible to imagine that Trevor could be a man inspired by, and walking alongside, the son of He who forged the universe. Trevor had experienced firsthand the ferocity and tenacity of God's love and he could no longer contemplate life without it. He might have wept over the decades spent living without this love in a fallen world, but the joy that now fueled him left little time for that. He might also have felt small, self-conscious and intimidated knowing he was traveling with the one who saved a world from eternal suffering, but Zac would have none of that. Much the way a young CEO returns home at the end of the day to laugh and wrestle with his kids, Zac was anything but self-absorbed. Trevor was at ease.

As expected, there was more at work inside of Trevor. He was quiet again, deep in a world framed by his thoughts. A curiosity was growing that was hard to quench. The love of God had changed his life, now he wanted desperately to understand more. There were many questions bubbling up to the surface, and he wasn't sure he could be patient enough to wait for answers. Trevor was fully aware of this facet of his person, but now, more than ever, he appreciated this quirk given to him by the hand of the Creator–the one who creates not by accident, but by design. As the two men walked, still bruised and scarred from the morning's confrontation, Trevor kept his thoughts to himself.

"Sometimes I can't figure you out," Zac said. "I've been through this patch of forest many times with a number of different people, usually by now they are peppering me with questions."

"I guess I'm not very inquisitive," Trevor said, straight-faced and bluffing.

"You must be forgetting who I am," Zac responded. "I know you better than you do."

The words gave Trevor pause. Years of convincing himself he knew exactly who he was, of trying to manufacture a complete being from the bits and fragments of attitudes and opinions he held tightly for reasons both good and bad, were exposed now. As much as his personality had flowed and morphed, there was always someone who could see past all of it, someone who saw the inner man that could never truly be altered, and the amazing potential that was too frequently camouflaged.

"You're probably right," Trevor said. "I thought I always knew who I was, but maybe not. I didn't have much insight into who you were either."

"How so?" Zac asked.

"I don't want you to get the wrong idea," Trevor said, "and please don't rain down lightning on me, but I would have thought you were a jerk—an unbending tyrant full of dos and don'ts, mostly don'ts, bent on choking the joy out of people. No fun. No laughter. No life. Just plain stiff, so much so, that even if I had believed in you, I would have chosen to live a different life."

"Don't feel the need to hold back," Zac said. They both laughed. "And how do you see me now?"

"I can't imagine trying to be like anyone else."

They hiked at a relaxed pace through most of the day. It was late afternoon when they came across a unique stretch of river carved into a series of small waterfalls, each stepping down gradually and forming a number of pools. Zac stripped down to his boxer shorts and stepped among the rocks until he found a comfortable nook in the falls. He settled into one of the pools where a gentle stream of water ran against his back. Before long Trevor joined him, soaking away the pain of a morning battle.

After some time in water that seemed much warmer than it should at this time of the year, both men climbed from the river onto one of the many boulders lining the falls. The rock was still hot from the day's sun and Trevor could feel his body warming and healing as he lay there. Each outstretched arm hung lifeless by his side as he watched the leaves of trees being swept back and forth by a light breeze that rose and fell.

"Sometimes it just feels perfect," Trevor said. He sat up, grabbed a handful of small rocks and started throwing them, one at a time, into the water, carefully watching the ripples. "I know you forgive me. I know you always will, but I was thinking about how I spent a lifetime trying to be tougher, stronger, more independent. I'm sorry I tried to do it again."

"I know you are," Zac said.

"But I still can't help wonder if I would have learned the lessons I needed to learn if I hadn't turned from you. Would I fully appreciate you if it wasn't for that time spent with Jacob and Jeremy?"

"Not everyone needs to stick their hand in the fire before they learn the flame is hot," Zac said. "I would prefer you learn your lessons without such pain, but if it can't be helped, a little pain now is better than great suffering later. The important thing is to learn."

Trevor's eyes looked up to a number of small yellow birds in the trees darting here and there from limb to limb. They weren't just birds anymore, Trevor considered them an essential part of creation, a unique and well crafted piece fit into the most elaborate puzzle ever conceived. They captured Trevor's imagination as he tried to comprehend what part they played in a much larger plot, and as he tried to discern the thoughts of the Master Engineer, his mind soared to new heights.

"I've been thinking a lot about my dad, who he was, how he treated me. I think he did a lot to turn me away from you. I was learning when I was young, but all the wrong things."

"He traveled a hard road," Zac said. "Sometimes the pain of a single life cuts across several generations. Sometimes healing never occurs when it should. I'm sorry you had to deal with that. I'm also sorry your father felt the same kind of pain. He wasn't as strong as you and it tore him apart. It fractured and compromised every part of his being, destroying every relationship in the process."

Trevor was silent. For the first time, he imagined his father as a small boy full of hopes, dreams, and desires. Trevor could see the wide eyed enthusiasm of youth beaten down by yet another embittered man; a man whose life came up short in the eyes of others, as well as his own. Trevor wondered how many tears his father shed trying desperately to understand why the man he loved most returned that love with anger and disgust. He drew a deep breath and dared to hope that things turned around for his father during the final years of his life, the years they were no longer communicating.

"Will I ever see him again?" Trevor asked.

"That depends on your decision," Zac replied.

"Is he in heaven?" Trevor asked.

"You will know soon enough."

"Riddles can be hard to live with sometimes," Trevor said. "I really hope he made it. As much as I hated the guy, I think I loved him too."

Zac nodded. Trevor laid back on the rock. Minutes passed in silence.

"I keep thinking about the pain question," Trevor said.

"Pain question?"

"Yes," Trevor said. "How can people believe in an all-loving God in a world filled with so much pain? It makes people—it made me think you don't exist."

"Yeah," Zac said. "It's a hard one, and yet, for all that pain and suffering, they tend not to believe in the evil one either."

"You're right," Trevor said. "I never considered that. You know, I lived as stubborn as a mule for more than 40 years. I finally meet you and my life gets turned around in little more than a week. Do you ever think about going back to earth? You could help people get to where they should be. Help them figure things out, see things straight. Wouldn't it be easier that way?"

"I never left," Zac said, "I know it may sound vague or abstract, but I really do dwell in the heart of every believer. They can call on me anytime. I am there for them. Lives are still changing, and those who want a relationship with me can always have it."

"But what about the people who don't believe?" Trevor asked.

"You mean the people like you?" Zac countered.

"Like I used to be," Trevor said with a smile. "Yes. I didn't have a clue. Nobody ever told me." He paused. "Okay, maybe that's not entirely true. But I never heard a single word about you from anyone I respected."

"And how many people did you respect?" Zac asked. The two men laughed.

"But seriously," Trevor continued, "if this whole journey had never happened, I would have never had a clue about who you really are, and who I wasn't. I would have had everything all wrong."

"What's important is that this journey did happen," Zac said. "I don't have time to explain to you the many different ways I have reached out to my people, hoping desperately to get through to them.

What I can tell you is that before the eternal die is cast, I will have found a way to make myself known to every man, woman, or child, and I will let them choose."

"Thank you," Trevor said as sincerely as he could. "Thank you for bringing me here, for teaching me, for being patient with me when I was a total idiot, for sharing, protecting. Thank you for saving me. I did so much to push you away, for so many years, and still you kept on."

"Like I said, I was there on day one. I watched as the fabric of your person was knit together, the intricate stitching and unique stylings, the limitless potential. I loved you deeply. I wanted to spend eternity with you, but like most, you didn't understand. You were caught up in a world that didn't know me. But I felt, despite the rejection, if you were given the chance to get to know me, if you really understood who I was—what I thought and how much I loved you—that you would want to spend eternity with me too. That's why I didn't tell you who I was back there in the mountains. You needed time to get to know me, something you wouldn't have allowed if you heard the name Jesus."

"It' just amazing you didn't give up," Trevor said. "I'm pretty sure I would have given up."

"There are parts of me you will never understand while trapped in that body of yours., but from the first day of your existence until the day you cross into heaven or hell, I will seek after you—each of you. Like a love crazed man chasing the affections of a beautiful woman, or a mother protecting her child, I will follow hard, tirelessly, hoping that somehow you will understand how we fit together. That is who I am, and that will never change."

Trevor heard the sound of water over rocks. At first it seemed faint and distant, but gradually it grew. He blinked his eyes several times and realized he had fallen asleep. It was obvious to him that the day was ending and night would soon be here. He stood up slowly, stiff from sleeping on a hard surface, and noticed the boulder beneath him had cooled considerably. He stepped down and saw an arrow on the ground, drawn from small rocks.

*He thinks of everything.*

Trevor stopped. Something felt odd. There was a strange dampness in the air, and life felt heavier than it should. He sat down upon a rock and a shadow seemed to move over his heart.

"Is everything okay?"

The voice startled him, but as he looked away from the river he could see Zac walking toward him. "I wasn't sure you would see the arrow."

"I never knew I could miss her this much," Trevor said.

He had lived with his wife for decades, but she was gone now, or he was gone. There would be no more goodnight kisses or the daily comfort of knowing she was there with him. He first started to notice the void after he moved onto the farm, and there were some moments when the pain was greater than others, but tonight's hurt was deep. He wanted to see her smile, hear her voice, or tell her a corny joke and watch that look of rehearsed exasperation settle on her face. He knew the distance between them was too great, that there was no crossing the chasm, and it only made things worse.

"I'm sorry," Zac said.

"I know. It wasn't the best marriage on the books, but we still did a lot together. She was my project buddy, my dinner companion, fellow movie critic, my co-pilot. I miss my best friend. I miss my wife."

"She misses you too," Zac said. "There were things you did wrong in your lifetime, but marrying Cindy was not one of them. She was, and continues to be, a good woman, a quality woman."

"I know," Trevor said. "I guess that's why I miss her so much."

"Come on," Zac said in a soft voice. "I've got some dinner ready, and I want to hear about how you two met."

"I'd like that," Trevor said, following Zac away from the river. "I think just talking about her will help."

"I think you're right."

They moved through a patch of forest and into a clearing, spending the next few hours talking about marriage in a way that Trevor had never considered; less about him and more about her. It made sense, but Trevor was acutely aware how selfish he could be, even with the best of intentions. It was too late to change things now, but at least he understood the plan, and he was thankful for that. He laid down to sleep, thinking about his wife, somehow feeling closer to the woman he loved.


Trevor's eyes opened and gradually focused on the stars above. Rather than fight being awake, he lay still, staring into the cosmos. He scoured the sky hoping to see Orion's belt, but it could not be found. These stars were different, grouped in constellations quite unlike those he had viewed from Earth. Realizing he had been tucked into a different corner of the universe, Trevor began thinking on its immeasurable dimensions. Then he wondered what heaven might be like, and where it might be. Trevor looked over to see if Zac was lying on the ground nearby. He wasn't.

*Not again.*

He stood up and surveyed the field surrounding him. With only a small amount of starlight, he quickly convinced himself that Zac was nowhere to be found. Trevor began walking across the field and then suddenly tripped. Zac hopped to his feet and stood before Trevor.

"You okay?" Zac asked.

"Yes," Trevor said. He gathered himself and looked in Zac's direction. "What are you doing?"

"Sometimes I don't sleep well either," Zac said. "Sometimes I feel a gentle tug on my heart, or a quiet voice in my ear, and that's usually a good time for me to pray."

"Why would you have to pray?" Trevor asked.

"To stay connected," Zac said. "We all need it, even me."

"But what is it you pray for?" Trevor asked.

"Tonight it's Jacob and Jeremy," Zac said. "Two guys with hearts as big as their shoulders are broad. They just let things sour along the way."

"You're kidding, right?" Trevor asked. "After everything they did to us?"

"Not everyone recognizes their mistakes," Zac said.

146

"I know," Trevor said in a humble voice. "It just sounds difficult."

"Can you try?" Zac asked. "I am certain it will do all three of you good." In many ways, Trevor felt unprepared to intervene on behalf of those who hated him. He didn't care that much. He wasn't that good. Still, Zac would not have asked if it wasn't important.

"I don't even know how," Trevor said, embarrassed.

"Just imagine sitting on the beach with a friend, staring at the ocean," Zac said. "But this is God, so you can toss out any ideas of being phony. He knows you. He wants honesty. You might want to tell Him how amazed you are at His creation, or thank Him for some of the blessings He sent your way. Maybe talk about your struggles, or ask Him for some help for yourself, the ones you love, or even your enemies. Just talk to Him, and when you run out of things to say, be quiet and listen."

Trevor lowered his head. He felt awkward, unpolished, even a little stupid, but he was glad to finally reach out to God in this way. There was much to be said and Trevor bared his soul to the heavens. By the time he lifted his head, light filled the sky. It was still early, and Trevor had lost sleep, but somehow he still felt refreshed. He looked over to find Zac gazing off to the west.

"We're getting pretty close now," Zac said. "Not much time left. There are still a few things I need to teach you."

"Was my life a waste?" Trevor asked. "Did I have a positive impact on anyone? Because from where I stand, I can't see it."

"Hard to say, because from where I stand, your life hasn't begun yet."

# 15

# Riverside

If Riverside was anything, it was a good community, willing to take care of its own. On this morning at 6:45 there were already six men ready to work. Some wore blue jeans, others wore overalls, but everyone's shirt was made of flannel. They were gathered in the yard behind Ethan's house, a tiny salt box structure surrounded by plenty of land. The men were standing near a pile of wooden rails and posts. Their hands were calloused, their wills were strong, and their hearts were open.

Samuel was giving out instructions when Zac and Trevor strolled up. "Good morning Zac," Samuel said. "Didn't expect to see you here."

"Seems we stumbled in at just the right time," said Zac.

"Or the absolute wrong time, depends on your perspective," Samuel said. "Who's this?"

"Everyone, this is Trevor. Trevor, this is Samuel, Caleb, Brian, Matt, Lee and Henry."

A chorus of "Mornin'" filled the air and everyone reached out for a handshake.

"You here to help, or just passing through?" Matt asked.

"I'd like to help, but I have an errand to run," Zac said.

"Would it be okay if Trevor pitched in?"

Trevor's eyes grew large but he held his tongue. He wondered what he was in for. His last work stint didn't go very well and he still had the bruises to prove it.

"Ain't no need askin'," Caleb said with a slow Southern drawl. "Every pair o' hands is like a little piece o' God, and we ain't turnin' that away."

"Good," Zac said, nodding approvingly to Trevor. "What's today's project, and what have you guys done with Ethan?" Zac asked, winking, and then leaning over to pick up a rail.

"That crazy old timer came out here in the middle of the night because he heard a wounded animal," Samuel said. "Fell right off the ledge. Broke his arm pretty good. He's been healing up back at Gary's. We want to get this fence put up before he comes home this afternoon. Should have been done three days ago but good luck tryin' to get this crew together. Soon as he gets back we're plannin' a big feast. How do you like barbecue, Trevor?"

"We don't get much in Jersey," Trevor said, "but I still remember how good it tastes washed down with a glass of sweet tea." The six men moaned with approval.

"Don't worry about a thing," Samuel said to Zac. "We'll take good care of him, and set him up with a nice dinner as well."

"Thanks," Zac said, shaking hands with Samuel. "I should be back before sundown. Trevor, don't let these fellas' push you around too much. I'll see you tonight."

"Sounds good," Trevor said.

By the time Trevor took his eyes off Zac's retreat, some of

the men had already begun moving lumber. Samuel grabbed a small piece of rope and a shovel. "Why don't you come with me?" he said to Trevor.

The two men headed to a slate walkway that ran from Ethan's house to a small ledge overlooking the river. From there a natural stairway, formed from large rocks, made its way down to the river. It was easy to imagine how a simple misstep could send someone over the edge. Samuel used the shovel to carve a small hole on either side of the walkway. These marked the first two fence posts. Then, using the rope as their guide, they measured and marked eight additional holes in each direction. By the time they finished, all the posts and rails had been moved into position. Now it was time for the hard part.

"I'll take Trevor, Lee and Brian," Samuel said. "We'll work this side of the fence. When we're a little past halfway we'll send Trevor your way. Does that work for everybody?"

Everyone nodded, and then each team picked up a steel bar, as well as a tool Trevor had never seen before. He assumed it had something to do with digging a hole, but he wasn't sure how. With an odd looking end that looked like two shovel blades joined together, it was anyone's guess how this tool could dig a hole. They all made their way to their respective ends of the fence.

Samuel made the first blow. He drove the steel bar into the ground a number of times, and then knelt down to liberate a pair of shoe-sized rocks from the ground. Lee dropped the mystery tool to the ground and started twisting it. Trevor immediately realized the tool was more of a drill than a shovel. Each time the opening between the blades would fill with dirt, Lee would lift the tool and drop the fill onto an ever growing pile. At some point his progress was halted.

Brian handed the bar to Trevor. "Rock," was all he said.

Trevor understood and started chiseling away at the hardened dirt at the bottom of the hole. Eventually he was able to free a rock not much larger than his hand. Brian started drilling, taking the hole to more than a foot in depth before the next barricade got in the way. Samuel grabbed the bar, made quick work of removing a considerably sized stone, and then Lee started drilling. The men quickly found their rhythm and each seemed to anticipate his opening before a word was spoken, but that didn't prevent the continual banter of men at work.

"Why do you think he never put a fence here?"

"Maybe he had too much on his plate."

"Could be. Maybe he's just lazy."

"Ethan? Lazy? I don't think so."

"He must have had a reason."

"Why don't you ask him? Maybe he didn't want a fence."

"You don't think he's gonna' get mad about this, do ya'?"

"I've known Ethan nearly 20 years. Never seen him get mad."

"You're right about that, he's quick to listen and slow to anger."

"But everyone gets angry sometimes."

"Stop your worryin'."

"If we ain't about worryin', then why we puttin' up this fence?"

It was like music to Trevor's ears—the unmistakable sound of friendship. He didn't say all that much, mostly because he enjoyed listening, but whatever he had to say was well received. Prior to this morning, Trevor had no idea who Ethan was, or any of the other six men he was working with. In the old world this would have been exactly the type of situation he avoided, yet now he was having a good time working with men who became friends at little more than the price of a hello.

"Are you a farmer too?" Lee asked Trevor.

"No, I worked in an office for a long time."

Lee grabbed one of Trevor's hands and examined the calluses. "You sure about that? You don't look like no office worker to me." Trevor's face lit up.

On and on they continued. After a little more than two hours with a few short breaks, they had finished digging five holes to a depth of 36 inches. Now it was time to make the switch. The other team was still working on their fourth hole when Trevor joined them on the other side of the walkway.

"It's about time," Matt said as Trevor arrived, and handed him the drill. Trevor grabbed the tool, dropped it in place, and hustled to finish the hole. His will had always been forged of iron, strong and unbending, and now he found himself motivated by a similar group of hard working men. But this felt much less like competition to Trevor, it was more like teamwork. His shirt was covered with dirt and sweat. Still he kept on.

The second group of men worked differently than the first. They, like the others, shuffled from man to man and tool to tool in order to keep everyone as fresh as possible. But this group had much less to say. It was several minutes before someone finally spoke.

"So where did Zac head off to?" Henry asked.

"Not–really–sure," Trevor said, separating each word with a half spin of the drill.

"I–under–stand," Henry said, using pauses to tease the newcomer. Trevor stopped to look at the older man and then everyone started laughing. "He's always got something to do, but the funny part of it is, he never makes you feel like he doesn't have time for you. You know what I mean?" Trevor nodded and went back to spinning the drill.

"The three of us have been diggin' holes, cuttin' trees, and plowin' fields together for a very long time," Matt said. "We know almost everything there is to know about each other, but we don't know nothin' about you."

Trevor stopped the drill again and thought for a few seconds. "I'd say I'm someone who recently woke up. Someone finally learning what it means to be alive." He began working the drill. "I guess that doesn't tell you much."

"Sounds like an earful to me," Matt said.

It was approaching noon when they finished the last hole. Everyone was exhausted now. Most of the wives were scurrying around Ethan's place making preparations for the afternoon feast. One of the women stopped by the work crew long enough to drop off a basket full of sandwiches and a pitcher of lemonade. Never had egg salad tasted so good.

By now, Trevor had a small glimpse of who each man was. He knew that Lee loved to talk about baseball and his favorite position was left field. Caleb had extraordinarily long feet for someone his height, but not as wide as they could have been. He laughed at some of the crazy stories told by Brian about things that would have made a great sitcom, and he already held a great deal of respect for Samuel after hearing some of the struggles he overcame as a young man. This was a community, and Trevor was feeling very much a part of it. The men had opened their lives, and by doing so, invited Trevor in to a place of comfort and safety.

Many of the calculations that Trevor was known to conduct about strength, intelligence, and determination were somehow left off from the day's agenda. He was spending less time being critical and more time listening, laughing, and enjoying the company of others. He was with friends now and there was no need to impress or intimidate. He even found himself willing to share a few chapters from his own life. There was talk about his first car, and the many off-road excursions before an axle failed. A story about a girl named Michelle who broke his heart back in high school when she left him for a guy that was two years younger than he. He spoke about some of the challenges he faced, and some of his aspirations as well.

After the lunch break the wives spent time outside setting up tables and chairs. The men worked together setting posts, sliding rails into position, and hauling dirt away. This kept them busy for a couple more hours, largely because distractions became so frequent. Seems as more and more neighbors made their way to Ethan's for the feast, several volunteer foremen wandered in, each inspecting the job and making sure to ask plenty of questions.

By four o'clock the men were all cleaned up, the feast was spread out over half a dozen tables on the side of the house, and a crowd of nearly 50 people were seated and ready to eat. All that was missing was the guest of honor. No sooner had Caleb snuck a piece of bread to hold back his appetite, when two horses stepped off the trail and onto the front yard. It was Ethan and Gary. As the horses walked toward the gathering, one by one, each person stood up and began clapping for their friend. At first it seemed cheap and shallow to Trevor, like a small child banging on a piece of sheet metal with a stick. But as more and more people joined in, the sound grew, as did the emotion, both eventually filling the yard. Trevor was moved by the tribute. Ethan, his arm still in a sling, remained on the horse until they finished. He looked around at his friends.

Gary had already dismounted by the time the crowd sat down. Ethan tipped his old, worn baseball cap, and with a little help from Gary, climbed down from the saddle. He walked to his seat, spent a number of seconds surveying the new fence, and turned to address his neighbors.

"I hate when bad things happen. I hate when bones break, houses catch fire, or floods get out of control. But I noticed over the years that those are the times when we really get to help one another. Those are the times when I feel the best about calling this place home. I love each of you like a brother or a sister, and I want to thank you." Ethan bowed his head and everyone else followed his lead. "Father, you know it's easier for me to put two pieces of wood together than it is two words, but I gotta' say somethin' here today. I want to thank you for this food, 'cause you know I love chicken and dumplings. I want to thank you for my neighbors, 'cause there ain't none better. Most of all, I want to thank you for being you. Amen." He looked up, took a deep breath while enjoying the moment, and yelled, "Dig in."

With that, plates and bowls began darting across the tables. Trevor mounded up large helpings of dumplings, pulled pork and corn, and then proceeded to devour all that his hands had earned. In between bites he listened to the conversations going on around him. Neighbors spoke about their children, farms, coworkers, the local store and whatever else was relevant at the moment. Some talked fast while others paced themselves for a marathon. Some were loud and some were quiet. Most interesting to Trevor, however, was that it didn't seem to matter who was speaking, or how loudly, there was no gossip or negativity. It was more than amazing, it was inspiring.

At some point between the dumplings and the peach cobbler, Ethan wandered over and tapped Trevor on the shoulder.

"I don't believe we've met," Ethan said. "My name is Ethan. I wanted to thank you for all your help."

Trevor stood up and shook his hand. "I was happy to do what I could. I'm Trevor, by the way."

"Yeah, I know. Some of the guys were bragging about how hard you worked today. Said if you weren't around they might still be at it."

"I doubt that," Trevor said. "It wasn't easy, but it was a lot of fun. I don't often get to work on projects like that, projects that really help someone."

"It sure is good to have a fence there," Ethan said, "and it really would have been nice to have one there last week. Oh well, no use crying over a few cracked bones. Any idea when Zac gets back?"

"He told me he'd be here before dark," Trevor said.

"I hope you two aren't planning on heading out tonight," Ethan said. "Can you stay 'til morning? I've got plenty of extra room."

"As you can imagine," Trevor said, "I'm not the one making plans, but I'll ask."

"Perfect," Ethan said, "and thanks again. It was a pleasure meeting you."

"It was nice meeting you, too," Trevor said. Ethan walked away and Trevor reclaimed his seat. He sat still for a few seconds gazing to his left and right.

"You don't belong here," a tiny voice whispered. Trevor turned quickly, hoping to see someone small and insignificant. Someone he could ignore. "You're not like them," the voice continued.

Somewhere deep inside Trevor knew the voice was wrong, but all he could think about was the small piece of truth wrapped inside a bigger and more elaborate lie. He was different. He had never lived in a place like this. He never experienced friendships like this. He could barely go 15 minutes without talking bad about someone. He wanted to kill the voice, choke the life out of it and bury it deep underground, but it was too late. A restlessness had already taken root and began to grow like a weed in good soil. Eventually all he could think about was finding a way out. He needed to be alone. He appreciated everything that was going on around him, and a large part of him wanted desperately to join in, to connect. He could hear the laughter, witness the joy, sense the closeness. These were good people and he knew they welcomed him without reservation, but Trevor could not be still any longer. Something inside, hidden so deeply that not even he could control it, demanded retreat.

And so, with stomach full and soul partly empty, Trevor rose quietly from his seat and walked slowly from the table, alone.

# 16

# Struggle

It was almost dark now. Trevor had found a secluded place away from the crowd and he felt safer. He sat against an old log at the edge of a field, watching the sunset. A long band of clouds stretched across the sky just above the mountains, leaving a tiny sliver of clearing between the two. Minutes earlier the sun could still be seen, but had since dropped out of sight. Now the cloudless strip of sky was on fire, a brilliant orange, and had a strange effect on the clouds above. Traces of purple could be seen where one might expect shadows, and accents of pink filled everything else. Trevor kept his eyes on the horizon, trying not to blink, wondering if he would ever see anything as magnificent again.

"Trevor?" a familiar voice called from the near the river.

"Zac?"

Zac hustled through the last of the trees and into the field. "What are you doing?" he asked.

"I was tired," Trevor said.

Zac said nothing. Technically Trevor's words were true, but they were also just a clever way to hide a much deeper struggle.

"I wanted to close my eyes and rest," Trevor said, "but when I got here I had to watch."

Zac sat down next to his friend and leaned against the log. The two men remained motionless, eyes set due west, neither saying a word as the orange glow slowly faded.

"There must be something wrong with me," Trevor finally said.

Zac sat in silence, inviting Trevor to continue.

"I just couldn't stay there," Trevor said. "I looked around and saw everybody else having such a good time. I wanted to be a part of it, to laugh, to smile, to not have anything to worry about or be frustrated with. I couldn't do it. I just felt so uncomfortable. I had to get out."

"I'm sorry," Zac said. "I thought leaving you with the others would be good for you. Maybe I was wrong."

"I don't know," Trevor said. "It felt so natural for most of the day, but something changed at dinner." Trevor scratched his leg and squirmed against the log. Every piece of him felt out of place. "Why can't I be like everyone else?"

"Is that what you want?" Zac asked.

Trevor wasn't sure if this was a trick question designed to reveal some flaw in his character. He didn't want to look like a fool, but he was also tired of second guessing everything and everyone. He wanted more freedom than that.

"I just want to be normal," Trevor confessed. "Is that too much to ask? I'm so tired of just walking away and being by myself. I want to find my place, wherever it is I can fit in, and stop being on my own. Please tell me there is something better than this."

"There was once a farmer who purchased a horse," Zac said.

160

"A handsome pony that could run like the wind. The farmer really wanted a good plow horse, but he didn't know much about horses and wound up buying a quarter horse instead. Over the next few years he worked the horse pretty hard pulling a plow, dragging trees, or hitched to a wagon. Not surprisingly, the horse never grew as strong or as thick as the farmer thought it should. He finally sold the horse to a friend who could see it wasn't meant for farm work. He wanted the horse for racing, but things never worked out there either, regardless of how much training was invested. The horse had been born for speed, but by maturing in an unnatural set of circumstances, it didn't feel right unless it was wearing a harness and trying to master some burden. But even though determined to work the fields, the horse's limbs and frame were never designed to handle such a heavy yoke.

"I was there. I saw what happened. I know exactly why you started trusting yourself and no one else, and if you want to know the truth—it makes perfect sense. It really does. But as logical as it may be, it doesn't make it close to being right. It's not the way things were meant to be. Fathers are supposed to love, and cherish, and sacrifice for their children. Children are supposed to grow up in the safety of that love, learning to trust, believing that another person really could want the absolute best for them. That, above all else, becomes the greatest example of my Father's love in the eyes of a child. Without that lesson it is far too easy to get lost."

"I'm never going to beat this, am I?" Trevor asked.

Zac stood up and brushed the dirt from his pants. "Come on, I want to show you something."

Trevor rose slowly to his feet. He felt better now that Zac was around, but he still felt very lost tonight. The two men picked their way through a thin patch of forest, and then followed a path along the edge of the river. It was slow going because they relied on a thin crescent of moon to light the trail.

They eventually reached a place where the river opened up into Blue Rock Lake. Zac pushed aside a number of tree branches and the two stepped onto a pebble covered beach. Although small for a lake, it was easily the largest body of water Trevor had seen since arriving at the In-Between. The water was still, almost like glass, and when staring at it for more than a few seconds it was possible to blur the line between water and sky. The reflection of the small piece of moon was perfect. Trevor's thoughts drifted until he heard Zac dragging something along the ground. When he finally looked over, Zac was dropping the front of a canoe into the water.

"It's even nicer on the water," Zac said.

Trevor moved to the canoe and hopped in the front. Zac pushed the canoe forward, jumped in and paddled onto the lake. The canoe cut a fine line in the water, leaving a very small wake. Trevor's head turned from side to side, trying to capture every sight, but somehow missed the island until the canoe beached itself. Taken by surprise, Trevor grabbed the sides of the canoe to keep himself from falling forward. The island, Blue Rock, was a massive piece of granite rising up out of the water. It was reasonably level in spots, but rose almost 20 feet above the waterline in others. Trevor instinctively stepped out of the canoe and pulled it further onto the island. Zac followed him onto dry ground.

Without a word, the two men proceeded to climb the rock. Standing that high above the water offered Trevor a much different perspective. The lake, still and black, now looked cold and lifeless—a thick ring of darkness separating the island from land.

"This is how you chose to live," Zac said. "Insulated. Protected. Isolated."

Trevor was still and his breath was shallow. Memories filled his mind. He looked out over the water. What a shallow existence it had been, so removed from friendship and intimacy.

"I didn't even realize what I was doing," Trevor said. "I was just trying to survive. It was all I knew."

"I understand," Zac said. "And so you fought, and because of your great strength you fought well. You overcame every challenge and heartache. But what you never caught a glimpse of was how much I had planned for you. There were so many lives I wanted you to impact, so many people around you that were hurting. You had much to give them, but pain brought pain, time after time. So you pulled away to protect yourself from the world after all the suffering it had brought you, and in the process, your actions kept you from doing so much of what I wanted you to do."

Trevor stared hard at the dark lake. He seldom spoke about his childhood.

"I used to play baseball when I was young. One day, I was probably about 11, our game ended and I looked around to find my dad. He was nowhere to be found. I don't know what kids are supposed to do in a situation like that, but I started walking. It wasn't bad, a couple of miles at most, but those cleats made it feel a lot farther.

"I remember I stood outside the back door for a minute, confused. I couldn't get that three run error out my head. I kept replaying it over and over. I wondered if my dad had left the game because of an emergency. My mom wasn't feeling well that morning and I wondered if he had taken her to the hospital. I guess deep down I knew she wasn't at the hospital, just depressed, but I wanted there to be a reason for her pain, something she could go to a hospital for and have fixed in a couple of hours.

"I went to knock the mud off my cleats, banging them together like I always did, but there was no mud. It had all fallen out on the way home.

"I stepped inside and heard the television, which seemed weird because my brother and sister were playing in the backyard. I walked into the living room to see what was going on and there was my father, sitting in his ugly recliner that was off-limits to the rest of us. I was too young to know what to say, so I just stared at him.

"Eventually he looked over. He asked me if we won the game. I told him no, we had lost by a couple of runs. You know what he said? 'I didn't think you could come back after that error of yours.' I can't tell you how bad that stung. Made me feel a lot worse than I had already been feeling. I wanted to be defiant, say something to fight back, I just didn't have those skills yet.

"I asked him how my mom was doing. He told me he didn't know and that I should go check on her. Then he just turned his eyes back to the TV.

"There I was hoping he had left the game to take care of her,

164

but that wasn't it at all. He left because I embarrassed him. I learned a lot about my dad that day. That was a real watershed moment. I didn't say another word, I just walked to my room, closed the door, sat down at my desk and started thinking."

Trevor became silent. His eyes remained on the lake. Zac walked closer and put his hand on Trevor's shoulder.

"That sounds hard."

Trevor looked at Zac. "I blew it, didn't I?" Trevor asked. "I had my chance, wasted a life, and now there's no way to make things right." Trevor was shaking. He felt worthless. He wondered if this was Judgment Day, the day that his life would finally be evaluated and found wanting in so many areas. The day he finally got what he deserved.

"You really have no idea, do you?"

"About what?" Trevor asked. All that was clear now was his confusion.

"You can't imagine how impressed I am with where you have walked and who you've become," Zac said. "What has it been, two weeks? Think about all you've faced, all you've learned, and how much you've grown. How can a man who has never seen light understand what color is? How can a man who has never tasted forgiveness understand grace? You need to be certain of one thing, you can only be held accountable for the things you can change, but don't. After that, there is forgiveness—the sweet, all consuming force known as grace."

"But what good is grace if people don't change?" Trevor asked.

165

"Grace exists because people can't always change," Zac said, "not on their own. That's the work of the Potter."

"God?" Trevor asked.

"Yes," Zac said. "There's a lot of pain in the world behind you. There's even some of it here. If you can believe there is Someone who always had a better plan for your life, if you can hope that He still wants the best for you, if you can trust He is leading you there, then there is a place you can walk to where all the damage falls away.

"I'd like to tell you that you can be free now of all the flaws and imperfections that have plagued you. I'm just not sure you can find that freedom between here and the doorstep to eternity. I would have told you the same thing if you had asked me 25 years ago. You cannot make yourself a new creation. You cannot take what is broken and make it whole. He makes all things new. He heals the diseased. He restores the weary. He satisfies the thirsty soul. Eventually, He sets right what should have always been. Until that day, the struggle continues, but what a beautiful struggle it is, marching steadily toward perfection."

Trevor sat down on the rock, an ox without its burden. It was a strange sensation. "I wish I had lived a better life," he said.

"You made your share of mistakes, but you are mine now. I paid the ransom and I am never letting go. I will not spend eternity without you."

# 17

# Sacrifice

"Be wise," Ethan said. "Rely on what you've recently learned to make your decisions from here on out. You'll do fine."

"Thanks," Trevor said. They shook hands and then Trevor hustled to catch up with Zac.

It was a late start this morning, possibly due to a shared dread about the end of their journey together. Fatigue from a night full of talk and deep thought could have contributed as well. Whichever it was, neither man was up and moving anytime near daybreak, so after a long relaxed breakfast with Ethan they were finally on their way.

The terrain was changing as they moved closer to the mountains. The ground rose and fell in gentle waves, so that whether they were in fields or forests, there was very little time spent walking level ground. Trevor's legs had been made strong by two weeks in the In-Between, and although the frequent climbs did little to slow him, his curiosity made up for it. While among trees, Trevor periodically stopped to look up and study the tall trunks that surrounded him. He could see tiny cut outs of sky through the canopy, and even caught sight of an eagle during one of his distractions. While in the open, on several occasions, he would slow his steps, lift his head slightly, and steal a glimpse of what lay ahead. Trevor had always loved the mountains, but those feelings of awe and admiration were now replaced with intimidation. The thought of eternity, the never ending unknown, can be enough to persuade even the strongest of wills to linger.

"There really can be a happy ending," Zac said.

Trevor nodded and took one step closer to his destiny, daring to believe for a moment that everything could turn out better than he had ever considered.

The stones looked different on this side of the valley, closer to brown than gray, and the further they climbed, the more rugged the landscape became. Trevor seemed more aware of his surroundings than at any point along this odyssey. Even now, he wanted desperately to find a way to control his situation, to dictate each step before it was taken. He could feel the urge pulsing inside, trying to overtake him, but resolved to beat back the compulsion by trusting what he could not see. He would continue walking through a wild land that was unfamiliar, toward a destiny he did not know. Trevor had learned something about obedience, and the dull, steady pain that it can bring.

It was late afternoon when they stopped. They had found a small clearing among the trees where they could be comfortable and make a fire.

"Tomorrow will be the end of one journey, and the start of another," Zac said, pulling off his pack and setting it down on a large rock. "We still have a lot to discuss before then." He unzipped the pack and looked inside. "Nothing left. I think I'll try to catch a few fish."

"Isn't that hard without a fishing pole?" Trevor asked, but before he finished his question Zac held up a spool of fishing line with a hook attached.

"I usually plan ahead," Zac said.

Not surprisingly, there was a brook nearby that was found to be quite rich in trout. Within twenty minutes Zac pulled in three fish and Trevor had a fire raging. Their last dinner together would be a feast, which was ideal, because both men were quite hungry.

"Keep them by the fire," Zac said, handing the fish to Trevor. "It helps keep the scent down." Trevor took hold of the line, walked to the edge of the clearing, and started digging through the backpack with his free hand. After a few seconds of futility he put the fish down on a rock and then continued his search with both hands. Eventually he freed a knife, studied the blade, and decided it would be a good idea to sterilize it.

Trevor moved to the fire and dipped the blade into the flame. He pulled it back after a few seconds, and then repeated the process, in and out, several times. He was careful not to drop the knife, or allow the handle to be scorched, but his eyes were lost in the flame as he stood in an almost trance like state. Trevor's mind was dancing somewhere between this world and the next, imagining the unimaginable. What would it be like? Boys have their dreams—professional athletes, presidents, astronauts. Young men have their's too—wealth, power, prestige. As men grow older they learn to stop dreaming and face reality—mortgages, braces, retirement. But what do dying men dream about? As they stand near the doorway to eternity, hoping, believing, or knowing that the best is still ahead, what thoughts capture their intellect, refusing to let go? Trevor had missed his chance once before, death came too quickly, but now his mind could not be stopped. He heard a faint grunt nearby.

He removed the blade from the fire and noticed it was covered with carbon. He took a moment to wipe it clean, and then noticed the reflection of his face in steel. He was barely recognizable. The face was largely the same, somewhat leaner and scruffier than when his journey began, but there was definitely something different in the depth of his eyes and expression. The person just below that outer layer of skin had undergone change, nothing shy of radical transformation, closer to perfection. Another grunt filled the air, this time louder.

Trevor snapped out of his trance and looked around, only to find a bear cub snacking on the trout. "Hey," he yelled, running toward the cub. He was quick enough to grab a stick and swat the animal on the rear end to insure he would not be back, and the cub retreated as quickly as it could into the forest. Trevor kept after the young bear until he stumbled across Zac gathering firewood.

"That lousy cub got one of the fish, but it could have been a lot worse," Trevor said.

"I don't think so," Zac said, looking to his right. At that instant a 600 pound female bear stood tall on her hind legs and growled with every ounce of rage she could muster. She was more than 50 yards away but both men could see the muscles tighten under the brown fur as she prepared for the attack. Trevor was overwhelmed to find an animal so large and ferocious as close and angry as this. His joints locked up.

"Run," Zac yelled. It was barely enough to loosen Trevor's knees. The two men began sprinting through the forest. Most everything was a blur to Trevor. Trees rushed by. Limbs snapped. Obstacles were avoided before his eyes could identify them. Ankles twisted slightly, knees strained, and the flesh on their arms grew raw as tree branches tore at their skin. Trevor had no idea where he was or where he was going, speed was all that mattered.

Behind them the sound of a predator in full attack was growing. Quick heavy steps ripped up the forest floor. Loud strong breathing, like the snort of a bull, filled their ears. It was as if a tsunami of claws and teeth was chasing and closing steadily.

At first Trevor was all adrenaline, arms and legs pumping as fast as they could move, but before long he could feel his body tiring. His legs were not accustomed to this pace and his lungs were failing. Fear was overtaking him and as he faltered, both physically and mentally, he could see a gap between himself and Zac widening. Time slowed, the bear continued the hunt, and Trevor was reduced to a frightened child.

"Don't leave me," Trevor called out not knowing what else to say. Zac slowed his progress to a crawl, allowing Trevor to catch up.

"I will never leave you," Zac said. The words came with as much sincerity and conviction as his breathing would allow.

This gave Trevor a sudden jolt of energy and for a few seconds his legs were fresh again. It just wasn't enough. Gravity continued bearing down on him until he nearly tripped on a log in his path. Zac, far more aware of their situation than Trevor, could see

171

they were only moments from calamity. He had to try something. He quickly cut in front of Trevor and steered him on a sharp angle to their left. The bear tried to make a quick turn but so much weight could not be easily redirected. More angered than deterred, the bear let out a thundering growl and then kept up her chase in a new direction.

Trevor was really failing now. Zac continued by his side, fully aware of the inevitable outcome.

The bear, in full sprint, reached out her paw and caught the back of Trevor's calf. She barely touched his leg, but the claws sliced through his skin and brought him to the ground. He laid on his side, hands held over his face for protection. He was done. He said the most significant words he could find for a time like this. "Please God."

The bear stood tall again, growling one last time before the fatal blow, but then something remarkable happened. Through his hands and fingers Trevor could see the figure of Zac diving full speed into the chest of the bear. Zac could not produce enough momentum to knock the bear down, but he did cause the animal to take two steps backwards to recover her balance, and that delay was critical.

Zac's eyes were full of determination as he readied himself for the counter attack. He looked quickly to Trevor. "Know that I love you," he said. "Now run!"

The urgency of the final two words helped Trevor find enough strength to jump to his feet and start moving again. He was confident that Zac knew something, some means of escape or unseen power that would deliver them from this nightmare. Why else would he try to take down a bear and buy more time for the two of them? Perhaps there was a hidden cave nearby where they could find protection, or maybe a short cliff above a river where they could float safely away. Whichever it was, he was certain of safety. He was also much better off knowing his friend had not abandoned him. But the further he ran, not quite as fast as when he started, the more he sensed that something was terribly wrong.

Then he heard it. The angry, chaotic sounds of a wild animal in battle. Zac's grunts and yells as he struggled with a monster four times larger than he. The muffled growl of a bear whose mouth is full of flesh. The tortured groans of prey too overpowered to fight back any longer.

Trevor stopped, turning to find Zac both bloody and beaten, his shoulder shredded and in the jaws of the bear. Their eyes met, and with what little strength Zac had left, he called as loud as his broken body would allow, one simple word, barely louder than a whisper. It was offered with love and concern from one brother to another, propagating like a sonic boom across the space between them. It met Trevor with a force that nearly knocked him over.

"Run."

*Everything for my good. Everything out of love.*

The bear readjusted her bite around Zac's neck and clamped down hard. Trevor could hear the unmistakable sound of bones cracking, and in that instant both men were gone.

Night had fallen. Trevor was frantic. His mind fought to

reject what his eyes had seen, but kept replaying the scene over and over again anyway.

*How can it be? How can joy so pure and complete be washed away by such intense despair? This is the In-Between, why should death mean anything here?*

He kept moving, slowly, through a thick and unfamiliar forest. For all Trevor knew he might be circling back around to face the beast again.

*How much horror can one man endure?*

His steps were tired and sad now. He no longer felt the need to rest, and so he stumbled, tree to tree, throughout the night. Trevor used his hands and arms the way an insect relies on their antennae, sensing his way through the thick. He could feel the wound on his calf burning and throbbing. He was fully aware of the gnawing emptiness in his belly but it was no more than a mild nuisance, hardly a reason to stop. Even hunger had lost its grip. It wasn't easy, but He pressed on, driven more by a desire for finality than anything else.

Trevor was numb now. Every emotion depleted. He held fast to a strange belief that he was traveling in the right direction. That somehow, after all the confusion, he was able to reorient himself and head toward the mountains. It barely mattered anymore since he was much less confident about where to go once he got there. Zac had taught Trevor volumes while they traveled the In-Between. He taught him how to be a friend, how to hold his tongue, how to love, and how to be loved. The one thing that Zac never taught him, the thing that Trevor needed to know now more than anything else, was which direction to travel when he arrived at the threshold of eternity. That opportunity had been lost, or perhaps stolen from him.

It was difficult to know what time it was. Darkness and despair had a strange way of manipulating the hours. Trevor was exhausted. His steps grew shorter and less steady. He eventually tripped over a large rock, holding out his arms to break the fall, but still managing to crack his head against a dead limb on his way to the ground. It twisted his neck and caused a light in his head to flicker, and then go dark again. He laid there, refusing to move, feeling the warmth of blood as it ran near his eye. The pain to his forehead and the emptiness in his soul overtook him. Trevor wept. Never before had he desired so deeply to be dead and gone, to be finished, to exist no more, to lay secluded in the black of night where nothing was recognizable and everything hurt, and finally give up struggling. He imagined the peace of surrendering to the inevitable would be far better than the doubt and discomfort of continuing to fight. There was nothing left. Trevor was defeated.

# 18

# The Beginning

It might have been minutes or hours, Trevor couldn't be sure. He had remained collapsed on the forest floor for some time, chest heaving with sobs of sorrow. Eventually it left him as something began moving inside. A calmness he did not have words for. Perhaps it was the simple understanding that there was nothing he could do to change his situation. It could have been the inner strength God had gifted him as a child to cope with difficulties. More likely, however, it was the realization that the love which changed his life during the past two weeks was still very much alive. That somehow the strength, the wisdom, the patience, the generosity, and the love his friend had showed him would not die in the jaws of a bear—it would live on.

Then a single word lodged itself into Trevor's thinking. It certainly wasn't the first time this word formed among the electrical pulses of his brain, but unlike all previous times it abruptly and unmistakably altered the view of his present circumstance. The word held great promise, greater hope, and unshakable motivation for a battered soul. It was a word that had recently become synonymous with home, a word infused with significance, a significance Trevor could finally understand. *Heaven.* It couldn't be that far away, maybe today, maybe tomorrow. What Trevor wanted more than anything now was to be home, and although he had no idea where it might be or what it would look like, he was determined to get there.

Trevor rose to his feet. He made a quick inspection of the wounds he was aware of, and a few he wasn't. Overall, he was still very much intact. He set off again. The forest was dense here, but the beams of light from above provided evidence that his navigation had been sound. He continued forward.

In short time the forest evaporated into grassland. Not far, perhaps only a mile or two away, stood the foot of a mountain. Trevor found himself moving up and down across a series of foothills and from the crest of one he noticed a narrow dirt trail below. He was glad to have found some trace of humanity. He paused for a few minutes, looking back across the valley toward the mountains where his journey began. This would be his final chapter, and the beginning of an entirely new adventure. A mix of excitement and fear welled up inside of him.

Trevor set off again but his steps slowed in an attempt to warp time. He wanted desperately to find a way to disconnect from last night's events, or at least come to some resolution in his own mind, before heading off to eternity. Just as in his world he was not ready to move on, now he felt equally unprepared. It seemed obvious that there were still lessons he needed to learn. Zac had confirmed this.

Before long, Trevor noticed a small stone house just off the trail. It seemed odd to him, considering how untame things were in this region of the In-Between, but it brought some comfort as well. Perhaps whoever lived there might be able to help him on his way, or at least offer some advice about which way to travel. Trevor stopped in front of the house, wondering if this tiny cottage was a blessing or a curse. He surveyed the landscape hoping to draw some conclusions.

The structure was small by Trevor's standards, sized more like a garage than a house. There was a large front door made of oak, mostly gray now from years of moisture. Two small windows, one on either side, were each swung partly open. The building looked like it had been there for a very long time, but the mortar between the stones was still in good shape. The cedar roof was weathered with a hint of green where it lay shaded by a large tree, but there was no sign that it was failing. There was no lawn in front of the house, only garden, overgrown in some areas and with piles of brush in others, presenting a somewhat unkempt appearance. From what little Trevor knew of gardening he was able to make out a number of different vegetables, and perhaps three or four herbs. The small trees on the far side of the garden were loaded with pears and he was reminded of his hunger. Then he saw movement.

An older man sitting on a bench, mostly hidden from view by taller plants, rose to his feet. Although his hair was gray and his skin somewhat wrinkled, he seemed far from fragile.

"Is that you Trevor?" the old man called, making his way through the garden. Trevor had been in this land long enough to expect the unexpected. Barely aware of what he was doing he began walking toward the old man.

"Yes," Trevor said in a voice timid and cracking.

"I'm so glad you made it. I've been watching for you." The old man reached out a hand in friendship, grabbed Trevor's forearm with the other as they shook, and eventually pulled Trevor close, giving him a hug. As they separated the old man studied Trevor's face. "Are you hurt?"

"I'm okay," Trevor said. Questions filled his mind.

"Nonsense," the old man protested. "We need to get you cleaned up." He led Trevor to a black metal hand pump near the house. After a few quick pumps of the handle the water started streaming out, cold and clear. The old man took several cupped handfuls and spread them over Trevor's face and arms. He even knelt down and rubbed a handful against Trevor's calf. The effect was immediate and Trevor could feel his strength returning.

Trevor didn't know why, but found himself longing to talk to the old man about Zac. He wanted to tell him what a great friend Zac had been, and how much he had done for him. He ached to share his own stories too, those of both victory and failure.

"I was traveling with someone else," Trevor said.

"I know," said the old man, stepping closer into what Trevor had once considered his personal space. Trevor looked into the eyes of the old man hoping to glean some understanding. If this was just a casual acquaintance, the news of Zac's death wouldn't hit too hard. But if the old man, like Trevor, owed his life, spiritual and physical, to the man from the mountains, then the news would be devastating.

"He didn't make it because a bear—" Trevor began, but before he could finish the old man raised his hand to stop the bad news from coming. His demeanor changed from joy to sorrow. He walked slowly back to the bench and sat down. Trevor walked closer. Compassion welled up in him as he noticed the old man was crying. He knelt close and grabbed the old man's hand. The old man looked toward him and in those eyes Trevor could see timeless oceans of empathy and pain.

"That was my son," the old man said, wiping his tears. "I'm sorry he had to suffer so."

Trevor's first reaction was to hold the old man's hand tighter, because he too was familiar with the depth of loss over a friendship so rare. He could only imagine how much harder it must be for the father of such a noble man. Slowly, however, the realization dawned on Trevor that this was no ordinary being. This was the Author of history, the Creator of the universe, the Perfecter of love. Trevor stood, attempting to pull away due to fear, reverence and ignorance. God grabbed his arm, refusing to let go.

"It was my fault," Trevor said. "If I hadn't left the fish out then none of this—"

God raised his hand again, ending the confession before it could indict. "I won't have any more of that," God said. "I'm glad we didn't lose you." God stood and wrapped His arms around Trevor. "He loves you so much. We all do."

Trevor's eyes filled with tears. He buried his face deep into God's shoulder. "He's dead because of me."

"No," God said. "He died because he loves you. Because at that moment in time there was no greater way that he could show his love for you than to lay down his life. And although he suffered terribly, far greater is his joy in knowing that you were saved. His love, our love, is boundless."

"I don't deserve any of this," Trevor said. "I'm no good."

God pulled away just far enough to look into Trevor's eyes.

He wiped the tears that were working their way down Trevor's cheeks. "You cannot earn my love, you can only accept it or reject it. He wanted us, you and I, to be together. He gave his life for that very purpose."

God waited for the reply that He knew would not be forthcoming, and smiled in such a way that Trevor could feel the morning sun warming. He placed his hand on Trevor's shoulder like a doting father with his young child.

"Can you stay for breakfast? I would really love to spend some time with you."

All Trevor could do was nod. Language had escaped him. God turned and walked toward the house and at that moment Trevor became acutely aware of two things. First, he recognized how well God fit into this setting. The house. The garden. The In-Between. Perhaps this was true for God in every setting, but the magnitude of His presence was overwhelming. Words like omniscient, omnipresent, and omnipotent were beginning to have real meaning. Second, Trevor recognized his concerns were gone. He was no longer alone. Any fear, loneliness, or confusion as a result of last night's tragedy had disappeared. Peace overtook him. He felt as near to complete as he ever thought possible.

The back patio possessed a natural beauty, flat stones laid carefully in place, but instead of mortar filling the spaces between each stone, there were narrow patches of grass. The table, set to one side, had been cut, not milled, from a tree. It was thick and sturdy, so that by comparison, most picnic tables appeared as if built from toothpicks. There were no benches or chairs, only stools carved from logs about three feet high and two feet wide. They were notched and hollowed in such a way that they remained strong, while weighing far less than their original weight. Strewn about the patio, in an almost random fashion, sat a large number of planters that provided homes to flowers and exotic plants. There was color everywhere. Along the edge of the patio ran a stone knee wall and beyond that, more fruit trees. Further out, a canopy of forest rolled up into the mountains attempting to touch the sky.

"Have a seat Trevor," God said, while setting down a large tray filled with yogurt, fruit, bread and juice. "You look well."

Trevor looked down at his clothes. "You must be kidding," he said.

"Not at all. You were always a handsome man, but now you've got a healthy grizzled look about you. Go ahead, have something to eat."

Trevor jellied up a large piece of bread and poured himself a glass of orange juice. He was still quite thirsty from the previous night's ordeal, and drank through the glass in a single sip. God quickly poured him another.

"And there is something else different about you," God said. "There's a clarity in your eyes, something I haven't seen in a very long time. A look that tells me you are beginning to understand who you are, and why I made you. I think your time here has been well spent."

"I agree," Trevor said. "I've learned a great deal."

"Tell me what you learned," God said.

Trevor thought for a few seconds. "I've learned that things

are seldom what they seem. That there is often more going on behind the facade that we call reality."

"That's true," God said.

Trevor paused again before speaking. "I've learned that whoever I was or wherever I walked back in the old world, I would have found a way to fail, to somehow fall short of the man I was designed to be."

God nodded his head in agreement.

"But none of that matters. Because far beyond my ability to mess things up, is your ability to set them right. And that is the hope which holds all things together."

God smiled on his child. "Yes, this has been a very good experience for you."

Trevor spent several hours with God, listening, sharing, learning and thinking. It was a taste of what lay ahead and raised the bar of what real living was about. They laughed, cried, and spoke with an honesty that could only forge greatness. Never before had Trevor been so transparent or so intimate. There was something about being in God's presence that commanded sincerity. Trevor could barely remember the pain of his past.

Trevor stood in front of the house, just off the dirt path. God was near and the sun was high overhead.

"I'm glad we had the morning together," God said. "I've been wanting to do this for a long time."

"I don't even know what to say," Trevor confessed.

"I understand," God said. "I feel it too. I was really missing you." He wrapped His arms around Trevor and Trevor's arms tightened around his Heavenly Father. After what seemed too short a time, the two separated. "Do you know where you are going?"

Trevor shook his head with disappointment. "Zac and I were suppose to talk about that," Trevor said. "We just never had the chance."

"Do you know where you want to go?" God asked.

Trevor paused. He looked toward the mountains and spent a few moments lost in glory. Eventually he turned back to God with a smile on his face. "Yes I do," Trevor said. "Wherever Zac would have wanted."

God smiled. He grabbed Trevor by the hair on top of his head and shook lightly. "When you come to the fork in the trail, keep to the left and follow it over the ridge."

"Thank you," he said. He took three steps toward the mountain and then turned. "Will I see you again?"

"Everyday," God said. "For all of eternity."

"Incredible," Trevor said, and then let out a laugh. "I can't even wrap my head around that. Eternity." He started to turn, but then stopped himself. "And Zac? Jesus?"

"Yes," God said. "He will never be far from you."

Trevor face could no longer contain the happiness that was growing within him. He was beaming.

"I guess I had better get to it then," Trevor said, heading off at an excited pace.

After a few seconds God called out, "Hey Trevor." Trevor stopped. "I almost forgot to tell you. Cindy came through here yesterday. She was asking about you."

"Cindy?" Trevor asked.

"She was very excited to hear that you were on your way."

"But how?" Trevor asked.

"Some people take more time than others, and days here are not always like days there. She lived 83 years in the old world. They were years well spent, and she has many good stories to share with you. I imagine you have a few stories for her as well."

Trevor turned and started jogging along the trail. God watched closely and started laughing with the joy that only a father can know.

# Afterword

First and foremost I need to be very clear about one thing—this is a book of fiction, not a book of theology.

Jesus has done amazing things for us. He stepped into our world to love us, to heal us, and to teach us. He set in motion God's new covenant, freeing us from a law that was too great a burden to bear. He allowed himself to be unjustly condemned and crucified, so that we might have a relationship with his Father. He loved us unselfishly all the way to His grave. Considering the magnitude of that love, is it reasonable to consider that, if need be, He might follow us into our grave as well?

I understand that some may read this book and consider it heresy. After all, what if people consider the idea of a second chance as a license to have a free for all here on earth? I believe Paul addressed this possibility very well in Romans 6:1-2;

*What shall we say, then? Shall we go on sinning so that grace may increase? By no means!*

The storyline chosen for this book was just a vehicle to tell the story of God's unconditional love for His people, and what might happen if even the hardest of hearts were allowed one or two weeks with Jesus. This is not theology, but for the sake of those who have been hardened by life's journey, refusing to believe in a God who continues to love and pursue them, I desperately hope it's true.